Anonymous

The Way of Truth
Or, a mother's teachings from the Bible

ISBN/EAN: 9783337096847

Printed in Europe, USA, Canada, Australia, Japan

Cover: Foto ©Lupo / pixelio.de

More available books at **www.hansebooks.com**

THE
WAY OF TRUTH;

or,

A MOTHER'S TEACHINGS

FROM

THE BIBLE.

"'These my words . . . ye shall teach them to your children."
DEUT. xi. 18, 19.

LONDON:

TRÜBNER AND CO., 60, PATERNOSTER ROW.

1867.

ADDRESS TO MOTHERS AND TEACHERS.

For many years the want of simple Scripture-teachings, free from doctrines opposed to the Hebrew faith, has been felt by most mothers of the Anglo-Jewish community. It is earnestly hoped that the little work now offered to the public will partially supply this want.

The Reverend Chief Rabbi, Dr. Adler, having kindly perused the MS. copy of these pages, and expressed his approval, the writer trusts no further recommendation is needed, so she merely adds, that in this abridgment the endeavour is to preserve as closely as possible the text of the English version of the Bible, on account of its beautiful simplicity, and its being considered desirable to familiarise the ear of the child with the text in common use. Some slight deviations from it, demanded by the pure spirit of Judaism, have been made; for these the commentaries of Messrs. De Sola and Lindenthal and Dr. Raphael have been consulted; such passages as have been altered will be found marked with reference to the notes from which they have been taken.

Proper names and numbers, which are in many instances wearying to the memory of a child, and are not absolutely necessary for the clear comprehension of the Bible history, have been omitted, as also some chapters and passages fitted for maturer years.

The conversational style has been adopted in preference to that of "questions and answers," for three reasons; firstly, that arrangement has been found more attractive; children fancy they are really listening to the expressed ideas of other children, and like to compare their own thoughts with those of their imaginary companions; they are thus led to reflect, and the facts are more vividly impressed upon their memories by the interest thus awakened.

Secondly, this form gives more scope for questions and answers through the medium of "Mamma," which would not spontaneously arise in the minds of children; on this account also, children of different ages, namely, six and twelve, are assumed to take part in the conversations.

And, thirdly, this form will, in succeeding portions of the work,* give more ample opportunity for explaining the observances attached to our festivals and ceremonies.

The compiler of this little work suggests that it should not be made imperative upon the pupils to learn by rote the whole of the "Conversations"; it may be well to commit to memory the simpler interrogations and the replies, but certainly not the longer explanatory chapters.

Many queries may be put by children that the

---

* It is proposed to continue the remaining books of the Pentateuch, and possibly through the whole of the Bible, in the same form.

instructors may not find answered in these chapters; it has been the desire of the writer to avoid raising any doubt that could not be entirely dispersed, yet fully believing that with faith and patient study, all may be made as clear as possible to our finite understandings, and should be answered to a child by deferring to riper years and fuller knowledge.

Although no question occurs in the "Conversation" on the third chapter of Genesis as to the potency of the serpent, the teacher is strenuously advised to explain the Jewish acceptation of the incident.

Children cannot mix with the Gentile world without having forced on their apprehensions the existence of evil spirits, from "Bogey" upward to that mightier worker of evil, who, according to the Nazarene creed, is impersonated by the "Serpent."

The experience of the writer has taught her, that children should not go unprepared to meet what to them is either, a novel idea, or forced upon them by wily conversionists, as an accepted fact, in the Bible.

The desire of the writer is to make the study of the Bible a pleasant pursuit. She fully believes that most children earnestly love "truth," and prefer the Bible even to their "story books," because they know it contains only truth.

The preface for little readers indicates the spirit in which the study of the "Word of God" should always be pursued, by a "mother and her children."

Unless from unavoidable circumstances, religious training should never be deputed to strange teachers.

Chiefly from a mother's lips should a child receive religious instruction; by her tender care should be fostered those sacred feelings which arise in the heart; from her loved precepts the child learn the first lessons of duty, and be led in the path of virtue. The writer offers no apology for presenting this volume to the public; she hoped that long ere this some abler pen would have accomplished the task; her only desire is to help those who would fain pursue the path of instruction, but who for lack of aid hesitate.

INTRODUCTORY CHAPTER

FOR

LITTLE READERS.

———◆———

THE compiler of this little work thinks that her young friends will like an introduction to the family for whom it was arranged.

Let them then fancy themselves in a pretty neat breakfast parlour; there, seated at a table whence the breakfast has just disappeared, are a lady and two little girls, two boys have just left the room on their way to school, and Papa has also gone to his business. Nurse and baby (for the youngest child is still called baby, although he is nearly three years old) are waiting for Esther. Baby is always brought down from the nursery to see Papa before he leaves home, and until this morning it has been the custom that Esther should go up with nurse and baby, leaving Ada and Mamma to spend the morning together.

Little readers, do you not wish for a description of the Mamma? Your friend, who now addresses you, hopes that there are very few who read this volume, who are not blessed with a dear, kind Mother. Any who may unfortunately have been deprived of this blessing, know how they have longed for it, or missed the dear one taken from them, and can well imagine what a good kind Mamma is like.

Ada is a girl of about twelve years of age, a nice, tidy, industrious girl. Her needle is already in her hand, for she will have to wait a short time before Mamma begins their usual morning chat. We will not call these chats lessons, as lessons have become associated in our young friends' minds with tasks, which often give as much trouble as pleasure; and Mamma's chats, although on serious subjects, were always looked forward to as being the most pleasant hours that her children spent during the day; for Mamma said, "I wish my darlings to love their God and His word as they do their parents," and she never kept the little girls a moment longer than they appeared pleased and interested.

Now, let us return to little Esther, a bright-faced, rosy-cheeked child, six years old. See! she has climbed on her Mamma's lap, her arms are round her Mother's neck, and she is coaxingly whispering something in her ears. We wonder what she is saying. When we hear Mamma's next words we may perhaps guess what has been Esther's request.

"Nurse, you may take baby upstairs; Miss Esther will remain with me this morning."

(Now nurse has gone; Esther is still on Mamma's lap kissing her, and thanking her for allowing her to remain.) "And so my little girl did not think I had remembered my promise," said Mamma, stroking her little daughter's head, and returning her caresses. (This promise was that Esther should remain with Mamma every morning for an hour as her sister had been used to do, and that they would read together a chapter or two from the Bible, and after having read it, talk for a little while about it. Mamma's promise had been made during the holydays, and the readings were to commence on this the first working day after סֻכָּה (Succous, or Tabernacle), so that they might begin the Bible about the same time of the year as we do in our Synagogues.) Mamma has now put Esther off her lap, and is telling her to place her little stool ready by her arm chair (Ada's work-table stands also beside it), as Mamma must go into the kitchen and make arrangements for her children's dinner.

Now, Mamma has returned, and is again seated. Ada's work is laid aside, and Esther is looking up eagerly to her dear Mother's face. We shall soon see how attentive she is, and how much she remembers of Mamma's teachings.

My little friends must not think that this is the

first time Ada has read the Bible (the Bible is a book which, although we read it through yearly, we may each time find some new lesson that we have not thought of before), neither is little Esther quite a stranger to the teachings of the sacred volume, but to-day she is about to commence her regular readings, and we hope to be able to accompany her in them throughout the five books of Moses at least. Perhaps we may also be able to learn the thoughts of our two young friends as they pursue their study to the end of the Holy Book.

READING I.

———o———

In the beginning God created the heavens and the earth.

The earth was without form, and the spirit of God moved over the waters.

And God said, Let there be light, and there was light. And God saw the light that it was good; and God called the light Day, and the darkness He called Night; and it was evening and it was morning, one day.

And God made the firmament, and divided the waters that were about it from the waters that were under it. And the evening and the morning were the second day. And God said, Let the waters be gathered together, and let the dry land appear.

And God called the dry land Earth, and the waters He called Seas.

And God caused the earth to bring forth grass, herbs, and fruit trees, after their kind; and God saw that it was good. And the evening and the morning were the third day.

And God made the sun and the moon. The sun to rule by day. The moon to rule by night; and the stars also. And the evening and the morning were the fourth day.

And God said, Let the waters bring forth living creatures and fowl that may fly above the earth. And God blessed them, saying, Be ye fruitful and multiply. And the evening and the morning were the fifth day.

And God said, Let the earth bring forth the living creature after his kind, cattle, and creeping thing, and beast after his kind, and it was so.

And God said, Let us make man in our image, after our likeness, and let them have dominion over the fish of the sea, and over the cattle, and over all the earth. So God created man, and God blessed them, and God said unto them, Be ye fruitful and multiply, and fill the earth and subdue it.

And the Lord God formed man of the dust of the ground, and breathed into his nostrils the breath of life; and man became a living soul. And God said, It is not good for man to be alone. I will make a help meet for him.

And God caused a deep sleep to fall upon Adam, and He took one of Adam's ribs and closed up the flesh instead thereof. And of the rib which God had taken from man made He a woman, and brought her unto the man.

And Adam said, This is bone of my bone, and flesh of my flesh; she was called Woman because she was formed from man.

Therefore shall a man leave his father and his mother, and shall cleave unto his wife, and they shall be one flesh.

And God saw everything that He had made, and behold it was very good. And the evening and the morning were the sixth day. Thus the heavens and the earth were finished, and all the host of them.

And God rested on the seventh day from all His work which He had made. And God blessed the seventh day and sanctified it. And there went up a mist from the ground and watered the earth, for God had not caused it to rain upon the earth.

And God planted a garden eastward in Eden. And God put the man into the garden of Eden to dress it and to keep it.

And God commanded the man, saying, Of every tree of the garden thou mayest freely eat; but of the tree of knowledge of good and evil, which is in the midst of the garden, ye shall not eat of it, for in the day that thou eatest thereof thou shalt surely die.

And God brought every beast of the field, and every fowl of the air, unto Adam to see what he would call them. And Adam gave names to them all.

CONVERSATION I.

Mamma.—What is the name of the first book in the Bible?

Esther.—Genesis.

Mamma.—What is the meaning of the word Genesis?

Ada.—Genesis is a Greek word, signifying history of the creation. The Bible was first translated into English from Greek, and the English translators retained the Greek names for the five books of Moses.

Mamma.—Can you tell me the Hebrew name for Genesis?

Ada.—Yes. It is בְּרֵאשִׁית (Be-*ri*-shees).

Esther.—What does בְּרֵאשִׁית (Be-*ri*-shees) mean?

Ada.—בְּרֵאשִׁית (Be-*ri*-shees) means "In the beginning."

Mamma.—You are quite right; but perhaps you do not know that the word בְּרֵאשִׁית (Be-*ri*-shees) is the first word of the first chapter of the Book of Genesis, and that all the books of the Pentateuch, or five books of Moses, as well as the weekly portions, take their names from the first principal word of the chapter or portion. Now, tell me, Ada, have you thought of the first lesson that may be learnt from our תּוֹרָה (*Thou-ra* or Law), as we Jews call the five books of Moses?

Ada.—I think the first lesson is that God formed all things.

Mamma.—Before we proceed, Ada, dear, tell Esther which are the five books of Moses?

Ada.—Genesis, Exodus, Leviticus, Numbers, and Deuteronomy.

Mamma.—Now let Esther tell me what God created on the first day, and the words as given in the Bible?

Esther.—On the first day God created light, and God said, "Let there be light, and there was light."

Mamma.—What on the second?

Ada.—The firmament, or the expanse, which we call the heavens.

Mamma.—What on the third?

Esther.—The earth and the seas, the grass, herbs, and fruit trees.

Mamma.—What on the fourth?

Esther.—The sun, moon, and stars.

Mamma.—What on the fifth?

Esther.—Fishes and fowls.

Mamma.—What on the sixth?

Esther.—Beasts, creeping things, and man.

Ada.—Mamma dear, we read, "And God said, Let us make man in our image." Does it mean that God is like a man?

Mamma.—Certainly not. We must have no idea that the Almighty possesses any bodily form, for we are strictly forbidden to imagine any likeness of Him. What we understand by these words is, that God breathed into man a portion of His own spirit, which we call soul, and which we believe lives eternally, that is, continues to exist when our bodies have perished.

Ada.—What is this spirit like, dear Mamma?

Mamma.—We can form no more idea of it than we can of God, whose image it is. All we know of the soul is, that when it leaves, our bodies become useless, and can no longer feel or move.

Ada.—Was there any other creator with God? for He says, "Let us make man in our image?"

Mamma.—No. We believe that our Almighty Father reigns alone without the association of any other power. The plural term, *let us*, is only used to mark the combination of all power in the Almighty. It is a common practice, even with earthly sovereigns, to issue their mandates in a plural form; thus an emperor or king will write, We command, etc. I wish you particularly to understand this, because people of other creeds may tell you that our Bible teaches a belief in more than one ruling power. Now, Esther, let me see if you remember what further we have been reading of to-day. Of what did God form man?

Esther. — Of the dust of the ground.

Mamma. — Tell me, Ada, the Hebrew word for Adam, and its meaning?

Ada. — The Hebrew for Adam is אָדָם (O-dom), from the word אֲדָמָה (Adomo), which means earth or ground.

Mamma. — Of what was Eve formed?

Esther. — Of a rib which God took from Adam whilst he slept.

Mamma. — What did Adam say when Eve was brought to him?

Esther. — He said, "This is bone of my bone and flesh of my flesh."

Mamma. — Can you tell me the reason we commence our days at sunset, and that our Festivals and Sabbaths always commence in the evening?

Ada. — Is it not because in reading the account of each day's creation we find written, "And the evening and the morning were the first day, or the second," etc.

Mamma. — Yes, my dear, and since you remember so well our texts, can you tell me which of our prayers is taken from this first chapter of Genesis?

Ada. — Yes, Mamma. The קִדּוּשׁ (Kiddush), or sanctification, for the Sabbath.

Mamma. — Can you repeat the words of this blessing?

Ada. — "And the evening and the morning were the sixth day. Thus the heavens and the earth were finished, and all the host of them, and on the seventh day God rested from all the work which He had made, wherefore God blessed the seventh day and made it holy."

Mamma. — Is this the whole of the קִדּוּשׁ (Kiddush), or sanctification?

Ada. — No. The blessing for wine follows, and then a thanksgiving for having given us the Sabbath as a day of rest, in commemoration of the work of the Creation.

Esther. — Why did God need rest? We read He only spoke to create all things; He does not work as we do!

Mamma. — I am glad you have asked this question. Your remarks are very just, my dear child; we are not to imagine that God needs rest, or that He is subject to any human feelings. We think God did not rest, as we should understand the word, but that He ceased to bring anything new into existence. It would appear that God fixed on this day in order to show us that it is proper and good for man to rest one day in the week, and that this day should be the one appointed by God.

Esther.—Did Adam and Eve work then, Mamma, in the garden of Eden?

Mamma.—We have reason to believe they did, for we read God placed them in the garden to dress it and keep it. What did God give Adam and Eve for food?

Esther.—The fruit of every tree and every green herb.

Mamma.—Was there anything of which they were commanded not to eat?

Esther.—Yes, they were not to eat of the fruit of the tree of knowledge of good and evil, which was in the midst of the garden.

Mamma.—With what punishment were they threatened should they eat thereof?

Esther.—God said they should die.

Mamma.—Who gave names to the beasts of the earth and the fowls of the air?

Esther.—Adam.

Mamma.—Now, my darling, go and play; you have remembered very well all we have been reading about.

READING II.

Now the serpent was more cunning than any beast of the field. And he said unto the woman, Hath God indeed said, Ye shall not eat of every tree of the garden?

And the woman said to the serpent, We may eat of the fruit of the trees of the garden. But of the tree which is in the midst of the garden God hath said, Ye shall not eat of it, neither shall ye touch it, lest ye die.

And the serpent said, Ye shall not die. For God doth know that in the day ye eat thereof, your eyes shall be opened, and ye shall be as God, knowing good and evil.

And when the woman saw that the tree was good for food, and that it was pleasant to the eye, and a tree to be desired to make one wise, she took of the fruit thereof and did eat, and gave also unto her husband, and he did eat.

And their eyes were opened, and they knew that they were naked; and they sewed fig leaves together and made themselves aprons.

And they heard the voice of God in the garden in the cool of the day. And Adam and his wife hid themselves amongst the trees of the garden. And God called unto Adam, and said unto him, Where art thou?

And Adam said, I heard Thy voice in the garden, and I was afraid, because I was naked, and I hid myself. And God said, Who told thee that thou wast naked? Hast thou eaten of the tree whereof I commanded thee that thou shouldest not eat? And the man said, The woman whom thou gavest to be with me, she gave me of the tree, and I did eat.

And God said unto the woman, What is this that thou hast done? And the woman said, The serpent tempted me, and I did eat.

And God said unto the serpent, Because thou hast done this, thou art cursed above every beast of the field; upon thy belly shalt thou go, and dust shalt thou eat all the days of thy life. And I will put enmity between thee and the woman, between thy seed and her seed. He shall bruise thy head, and thou shalt bruise his heel.

Unto the woman God said, I will greatly multiply thy sorrow, and thy husband shall rule over thee.

And unto Adam God said, Because thou hast hearkened to the voice of thy wife, and hast eaten of the tree of which I commanded thee, saying, Thou shalt not eat of it, cursed is the ground for thy sake; in sorrow shalt thou eat of it all the days of thy life. Thorns also, and thistles shall it bring forth, and thou shalt eat the herbs of the fields. In the sweat of thy face shalt thou eat bread till thou return unto the ground, for out of it wast thou taken; dust thou art and unto dust shalt thou return.

And Adam called his wife Eve, because she was to be the mother of all living.

And God made coats of skins and gave them to Adam and Eve, and clothed them.

And God sent Adam and Eve out of the garden of Eden, and He placed Cherubim at the east of the garden of Eden, and a flaming sword which turned every way to guard the way to the tree of life.

CONVERSATION II.

Mamma.—What do we read of the serpent?
Esther.—That he was more cunning than any of the beasts of the field.
Mamma.—How did the serpent tempt Eve?
Ada.—He told her that the fruit of the tree would make her wise, and that she would not die as God had said.
Mamma.—Did Eve yield to the temptation?
Esther.—Yes, she eat of the fruit, and gave also to her husband, and he did eat.
Mamma.—After Adam and Eve had eaten of the fruit, what did they?
Esther.—They sewed fig leaves together, and made themselves aprons.
Mamma.—What did Adam and Eve do when they heard the voice of God in the garden?
Esther.—They hid themselves amongst the trees.
Ada.—Was not this very foolish? Ought they not to have known that they could not hide themselves from God?
Mamma.—Had they thought properly they would have known that there was no place in which they could hide themselves from God; and I hope, my dear children, you will remember this. If ever you are tempted to do anything wrong, think that God can always see you, even when no human being is at hand.
Esther.—Is it not strange that God should have asked Adam and Eve what they had done? He must have known.
Mamma.—God knows everything, my dear child, both things that have happened, and that will come to pass; but in reading the whole history, as given in the Bible, we find that God deals with all human beings, and speaks to

them in language they can understand. By asking Adam what he had done, God gives him the opportunity of confessing his sin, thus, in a measure, repenting. Now, tell me, Esther, how did Adam answer when God asked him concerning his sin?

Esther.—He said, " The woman whom thou gavest to be with me, she gave me of the tree, and I did eat."

Mamma.—And when the woman was asked, upon whom did she endeavour to lay the blame?

Esther.—Upon the serpent.

Mamma.—How were Adam and Eve punished for their disobedience?

Esther.—They were driven out of the garden of Eden, and were compelled to labour hard for their bread. They were also told, that their bodies should return to the dust from which they were taken.

Ada.—Does it not appear that the punishment of Adam and Eve was very severe in proportion to the crime they had committed?

Mamma.—I do not object to your question, my dear Ada, although we should know that all God's decrees must be just. I am glad to find that you think about our readings. It is not always easy to understand God's ways, but in this instance I do not think that the punishment should appear to us too severe, when we consider that God had given to Adam and Eve everything they could desire, and had only commanded them to abstain from the fruit of this one tree, in order to prove their obedience to His will.

Ada.—But, dear Mamma, God did not give Adam and Eve the reason for his command.

Mamma.—Most truly he did not. What lesson does this history teach us? I see you have not thought of it. I believe it to be this, that we should at all times act exactly in obedience to God's law; and must on no account wait until we can understand the reasons for which commands have been given, but perform everything we find written in the law.

Ada.—Do you mean then, Mamma, that it is wrong to try to find out reasons for the commands God has given us?

Mamma.—By no means, my dear; in trying to discover the reasons for God's commands to us, we are sure to become more convinced of His goodness and mercy; many things which are not clear to us at first become so upon study. What I wish to impress upon you is, that we may be certain all God has desired us to do is for our own good.

Esther.—But, Mamma dear, I do not as yet know nearly all that the Bible teaches us to do.

Mamma.—For which reason, my darling, God has commanded children to obey and honour their parents; for your parents will surely direct you in all that is right. In the same way as Adam and Eve should have obeyed God so should you obey your parents. That is to say, do exactly as they tell you, even though you question their reasons after you have obeyed their wishes.

Esther.—Mamma dear, we have said nothing about the serpent.

Mamma.—You are a good girl to remind me of this before we finish our conversation to-day. Do you not remember how he was punished?

Esther.—Yes, he was condemned to crawl in the dust all the days of his life, and he was told "that there should always be enmity between his seed and the seed of the woman." Mamma dear, did all the animals speak in the time of Adam and Eve?

Mamma.—I cannot tell you, my dear. I can only speak *positively* of such things as the Bible tells us. It is quite possible that the animals spoke, for Eve showed no surprise when she was addressed by the serpent.

READING III.

AND God gave unto Adam and his wife a man child, and they called his name Cain. And again another son, and they called his name Abel. And Abel was a keeper of sheep, and Cain became a tiller of the ground.

And Cain brought of the fruit of the ground an offering to God. And Abel brought the firstlings of his flock and the fattest of them.

And God had respect unto Abel and his offering, but unto Cain and his offering God had not respect. And Cain was very wroth.

And God said unto Cain, Why art thou wroth, and why is thy countenance fallen? If thou doest well, canst thou not lift it up? and if thou doest not well, sin lieth at the door. Though its desire be unto thee, thou shouldst rule over it.

And Cain talked with his brother Abel, and when they were in the field, Cain rose up and slew his brother Abel.

And God said unto Cain, Where is Abel thy brother? And Cain said, I know not: am I my brother's keeper?

And God said unto Cain, What hast thou done? The voice of thy brother's blood crieth unto Me from the ground. And now art thou cursed from the earth, which hath opened her mouth to receive thy brother's blood from thy hand. The ground shall not henceforth yield the fruit of thy labour, and thou shalt be a wanderer and an exile upon the earth.

And Cain said unto God, My punishment is

greater than I can bear; Thou hast driven me from the face of the earth; and from Thy face shall I be hid; I shall be an exile and a vagabond, and anyone finding me may slay me.

And God set a mark upon Cain lest any finding him should kill him.

And Cain went out from the presence of God and dwelt in the land of Nod.

And Cain had a son and called his name Enoch, and he built a city and called it after his son.

And the descendants of Cain were Jabal, Jubal and Tubal-cain—Jabal was the father of all such as dwell in tents—Jubal was the first who taught men to handle the harp and organ—and Tubal-cain was the first who instructed men in the working of brass and iron.

After this, God gave Adam and Eve another son instead of Abel, and they called his name Seth.

And Seth had a son whose name was Enos, and the son of Enos was Canaan, and of Canaan Mahalaleel, and of Mahalaleel Jared, of Jared Enoch, of Enoch Methusaleh, of Methusaleh Lamech, of Lamech Noah.

And Enoch walked with God, and he was not, for God took him.

And Noah had three sons, Shem, Ham, and Japheth.

And Methusaleh lived 969 years.

And Lamech was old when his son Noah was born, therefore he called him Noah, which means the same shall comfort us.

CONVERSATION III.

Mamma.—What was the name of Adam and Eve firstborn son? and what his occupation?

Esther.—His name was Cain, and he was a tiller ot the ground.

Mamma.—What was the occupation of Abel, their second son?

Esther.—He was a shepherd.

Mamma.—What offerings did they each bring to God?

Esther.—Cain brought of the fruit of the ground, and Abel of the firstborn and fattest of his flock.

Mamma.—Were they both equally acceptable to God?

Esther.—No, God did not regard Cain's offering with favour. Why was this, Mamma? we have not read that Cain had done anything wrong?

Mamma.—Until we read that Cain and Abel brought these offerings, we have none of their actions recorded; but it is evident from the text which follows the account of God's rejection of Cain's offering—that God who "sees not as man seeth" knew that Cain did not bring the offering in a proper spirit, for if you notice we read further on, that Cain must have nourished some evil desires or passions, which God tells him he can subdue if he will. Can you not remember the words of the text in which God addresses Cain, when the latter is wroth, and his countenance fallen?

Ada.—Yes; God said to him, "Why art thou wroth? and why is thy countenance fallen? If thou doest well, canst thou not lift it up? and if thou doest not well, sin lieth at the door. Though its desire be to thee, thou shalt rule over it."*

Mamma.—I wish you, my dear children, to think well

* See Gen. iv. 7, with notes of De Sola, Lindenthal and Raphael.

over these words, and, indeed, over the whole history of the actions of Cain and Abel; we should never read of the actions of others without endeavouring to profit by them ourselves, to avoid the wrong and imitate the right. Can you tell me the lesson we may learn from the history we have just read?

Ada.—Will you tell us, dear Mamma? I have some idea, but I do not think I can explain it as well as you will.

Mamma.—Firstly, then, we may learn that if we pray to God, or give offerings of charity, neither our prayers nor our offerings will be acceptable to Him unless they are offered in a true spirit of thankfulness; or if they be sin offerings, unless we sincerely repent of our misdeeds; that is to say, try to amend our ways, and do better in future.

Secondly—we may learn, that although we may have evil desires, and feel tempted sometimes to do wrong, it is in our power to subdue our passions and act in accordance with the will of God. I also firmly believe, my dear children, that if we pray sincerely to God He will help us to do right. If you, Esther, do not quite understand what we have been saying, you will do so when you are older. Now, darling, tell me, when Cain was alone with his brother what happened?

Esther.—Cain slew Abel.

Mamma.—How did Cain answer when asked by God, Where his brother Abel was?

Esther.—He said, "I know not. Am I my brother's keeper?"

Mamma.—What further sin did Cain commit besides slaying his brother?

Esther.—He told an untruth.

Ada.—Was it not foolish as well as wicked of Cain to tell an untruth? God knew what he had done; for, as you have told us before, dear Mamma, God can always see us.

Mamma.—You are right, my dear, and I hope you will always remember this. I also wish you to think of the real fault which led to Cain's great crime, which was envy; Cain envied his brother because he saw that God favoured him; and, instead of trying to imitate him and become better himself, he was angry. We should all remember this whenever we feel the least inclined to be envious of others who may succeed better than ourselves. It is right to try to be as good as possible ourselves, but very wrong to try to make other people appear worse than they are, in order that we may be thought better. Envy is a sin we are apt to commit much oftener than we have any idea of, and we should be very careful to guard against it. What punishment did God inflict upon Cain?

Esther.—He forbade the ground to yield the fruit of his labours, and condemned him to be a wanderer and an exile.

Mamma.—What did God do to Cain to prevent anyone from killing him?

Esther.—God set a mark upon him.

Mamma.—The word "Nod" means exile; Cain then went into exile, and the land was afterwards so called from this circumstance. What do we next learn concerning Cain?

Ada.—That he built a city which he called by the name of his son Enoch.

Mamma.—What is remarkable of Cain's descendants?

Ada.—That Jabal was the first man who dwelt in tents, Jubal the first who taught the use of musical instruments, and Tubal-cain the first who taught men to work in brass and iron.

Mamma.—Can you tell me from which of Adam and Eve's sons the present human race is descended?

Ada.—From Seth, the third son, whom God gave to Adam and Eve, instead of Abel whom Cain slew.

Mamma.—Can you name the patriarchs who lived before the flood?

Ada.—Yes; they were Adam, Seth, Enos, Canaan, Mahalaleel, Jared, Enoch, Methusaleh, Lamech, and Noah.

Mamma.—Can you remember a son of Cain was named Enoch? This was not the same Enoch of whom we read, " that he was a good man, and walked with God, and he was not, for God took him."

Esther.—What do you mean, dear Mamma, by saying that Enoch walked with God?

Mamma.—It means, my dear, that he did all that was right and pleasing in God's sight.

Ada.—We are taught that Enoch was taken to heaven without dying, but I do not see that it is so written in the Bible.

Mamma.—The Bible does not relate this fact in words which we can translate into English plainly, but it does not say that Enoch died, as is said of all the other patriarchs. The words of the text are—" Enoch was not, for God took him." We therefore believe that, as a reward for his righteousness, God permitted him to enter another state of existence, without suffering the pain of death.

Esther.—Were there also two Lamechs, Mamma?

Mamma.—Yes, my dear; there was one the descendant of Cain, and another who was the father of Noah. Can you tell me the meaning of Noah's name?

Ada.—It means " the same shall comfort us."

Mamma.—Who was the oldest man?

Esther.—Methusaleh.

Mamma.—How many years did he live?

Ada.—Nine hundred and sixty-nine years.

READING IV.

———o———

AND when men increased upon the earth they forsook the ways of God, and became very wicked, and the earth was filled with strife.

And God said, I will destroy men from off the earth. But Noah found favour in the sight of the Lord.

Noah was a just man, and perfect in his generations, and walked with God. Noah had three sons Shem, Ham, and Japheth.

And God told Noah to make an ark of gopher wood, to make rooms in it, and to pitch it within and without with pitch.

And God told Noah the size he was to make the ark, and He told him to make a window in it, and God also told Noah how he should divide the rooms.

And God told Noah that He would bring a flood of water upon the earth to destroy all flesh; but that Noah, his wife, his sons, and his sons' wives, with pairs of every living creature, should be brought into the ark to be saved.

And God commanded Noah to take into the ark seven pairs of all beasts that were clean, and two of all animals that were unclean, and food to keep them alive.

And Noah did all that God commanded him, and went into the ark with his wife, and his sons, and their wives, and all the living creatures as God had commanded him, and God shut them in.

And all the fountains of the great deep were broken up, and the windows of heaven were opened.

And the flood was upon the earth forty days and forty nights.

And the waters bore up the ark above the earth. And all the mountains that were under the heavens were hid in the water, and all flesh died that moved upon the earth.

And Noah only was left together with those that were with him in the ark. And the waters were upon the earth one hundred and fifty days.

And after that time God remembered Noah, and every living creature that was with him in the ark, and God made a wind to pass over the earth, and the waters abated.

And the ark rested in the seventh month, on the seventeenth day of the month, upon the mountains of Ararat.

And the waters decreased until the tenth month; and on the first day of the month the tops of the mountains were seen.

And it came to pass at the end of forty days, that Noah opened the window of the ark, and sent forth a raven, which went to and fro until the waters were dried up from off the earth; he sent forth a dove also, but the dove found no place of rest for the sole of her foot, and she came back into the ark; and Noah put forth his hand and took her in again.

And he stayed yet other seven days, and again he sent forth the dove out of the ark, and the dove came in to him in the close of the day, and lo! in her mouth was an olive leaf, plucked off; so Noah knew that the waters were going back from off the earth.

And he waited other seven days, and sent forth the dove, which came not again into the ark.

And Noah looked, and behold, the face of the earth was dry.

And God said unto Noah, Go forth out of the ark, thou, and all that are with thee, and bring them forth, that they may increase and fill the earth.

And Noah did as God commanded him.

CONVERSATION IV.

Mamma.—Why did God bring a flood of waters upon the earth to destroy it?

Esther.—Because mankind had become very wicked.

Mamma.—Who alone found favour in the sight of God?

Esther.—Noah.

Mamma.—Can you remember, Ada, the words of the text in which we are given the reason that Noah was saved, when the rest of mankind perished?

Ada.—Yes, dear Mamma, we find written, that "Noah was a just man, perfect in his generations, and walked with God."

Esther.—What is the meaning of "perfect in his generations"?

Mamma.—By this expression, I think we are to understand, not that Noah was perfect, for there is no man who "doeth good and sinneth not," but that in comparison with the people amongst whom he lived he was perfect, which means that he did not fall into any of the sins that were common with them. "In his generations," I believe, means, in the time in which he lived. Have you thought of the lesson that may be learned from Noah's conduct, and the reward he received?

Esther.—Do you mean, Mamma, that we should always try to be good?

Mamma.—That is certainly correct; but this lesson we may learn by studying the result of any one of the Biblical characters. The history of Noah teaches us more especially to consider for ourselves, what is really right or wrong, and not to be "led by the multitude to do evil." Can you explain to us, Ada, in what manner the position of Noah was particularly trying?

Ada.—I believe you mean, dear Mamma, what I have

often thought of, namely, that Noah must have found it more difficult than we should, to do right, being surrounded as he was by people who were all acting wickedly, and whom I should fancy must have laughed at him for persevering in the right path, and most likely disbelieved that God had commanded him to build the ark.

Mamma.—You have taken exactly the view I desired of the subject. I am very pleased that you have expressed yourself so fully. I trust you will remember through life the lesson I am particularly anxious to impress upon your memory; that you will always persevere in doing all that you know to be right, and have sufficient firmness to carry out the precepts of the Bible and the instructions of your teachers, even if you should be thrown amongst people who may laugh at you for so doing, and ridicule those observances which you have been taught to consider as sacred.

Ada and Esther.—We will try, dear Mamma, always to think of what is right, and to remember all you tell us.

Mamma.—And if you feel inclined to do wrong, or are not quite sure of what is right when I am not near, and you have no kind teacher by to guide you, will you pray to God to direct you?

Esther.—But, Mamma, will the great God listen to the prayers of a little child like myself?

Mamma.—My darling, there is nothing too small or too insignificant to be cared for by our Almighty Father. He loves all His creatures, small as well as great, and I firmly believe will give us strength to do right, if we pray sincerely for His help. You must not think that God is unmindful of you if He does not grant your petition immediately; God knows better than we do ourselves what is good for us, and it is often in mercy that He does not grant us our desires. You know *I* love you, my darling, yet I am often obliged to forbid you many things you would like to do, and cannot always give you reasons for my commands; but we shall have further opportunity of talking about prayers as our Bible history advances. There is yet one great virtue Noah possessed that we have not considered—perhaps Ada can tell us what I mean?

Ada.—I think you mean, dear Mamma, the great faith he must have had in the truth of God's word to have commenced building the ark a whole hundred years before the flood was to take place.

Mamma.—Exactly, my dear. Now let Esther tell me the names of Noah's three sons who were saved with him in the ark?

Esther.—Noah's sons were, Shem, Ham, and Japheth.

Mamma.—Why is Shem mentioned first when he was not the eldest of Noah's sons?

Ada.—Because it was from him that Abraham was descended, and he was the forefather of the Israelites, of whose history the Bible specially treats.

Mamma.—How was Noah saved when the waters covered the whole earth?

Esther.—He was saved in the ark which God had commanded him to make.

Mamma.—What did Noah take with him into the ark?

Ada.—Pairs of every living thing and sevens of all clean animals and birds.

Esther.—What is meant by clean animals?

Mamma.—The animals which we are now allowed to use for food, and that were used before the law was given for sacrifice.

Esther.—How did Noah know when he was to leave the ark?

Mamma.—I think you ought to have been able to tell me this. Ada will do so since you forget.

Ada.—At the end of forty days and forty nights, Noah sent out a dove which returned to the ark; he then waited seven days, and again sent out the dove, which returned, bearing an olive leaf in her mouth. After having waited another seven days, he again sent out the dove, which returned no more, so he knew that she must have found a place to rest on.

Mamma.—How long did the rain continue to fall?

Esther.—Forty days and forty nights.

Mamma.—Did Noah leave the ark immediately that he knew that the earth was dry?

Ada.—No ; he waited until God commanded him to go forth.

Mamma.—What did God say to Noah and his family?

Esther.—He blessed them and said, Be fruitful, and multiply, and replenish the earth.

READING V.

———o———

AND Noah and his family went forth from the ark.

And Noah builded an altar unto the Lord, and took of all clean beasts, and of all clean birds, and did offer them upon the altar with fire unto the Lord; and God accepted the offering.

And God said, I will not again curse the ground for man's sake, neither will I again smite every living thing as I have done.

While the earth lasts, seed-time and harvest, cold and heat, summer and winter, and day and night, shall not cease.

And God blessed Noah and his sons, and said unto them, Be fruitful, and multiply, and fill the earth.

And the fear of you and the dread of you shall be upon the fowls of the air, and upon all that moveth upon the earth, and upon all the fishes of the sea; into your hands shall they be given.

Each moving thing that liveth shall be meat for you; even as the green herb have I given you all things.

But the flesh with the life thereof, which is the blood, you shall not eat.

And surely your own blood will I require, of every soul will I require it, and at the hand of every man will I require the life of man his brother.*

Whoso sheddeth man's blood by man shall his blood be shed.

And God spake unto Noah and to his sons, saying,

* See Supplementary Notes to Messrs. De Sola, Lindenthal, and Dr. Raphael's Genesis, Chap. ix., p. 52, note *d*.

Behold, I establish my covenant with you and with your seed after you, that all flesh shall no more be cut off by the waters of a flood, neither will I destroy the earth any more.

And God said, This is the sign of my covenant with Noah, and every living creature for ever.

My bow I have set in the cloud. And when the bow shall be in the cloud, I will look upon it, to remember the covenant between me and every living creature that is upon the earth.

And the descendants of Noah increased and multiplied, and journeyed eastward, and all the people of the earth were of one language, and they feared lest they should be scattered abroad over the face of the earth, and they said,

Côme, let us build a city and a tower, whose top may reach to heaven; and they made brick, and burned them. Thus they had brick for stone, and slime for mortar.

And when God saw what they had done He confounded their language so that they could not understand each other.

Therefore the name of the city was called Babel, and God scattered the people over the face of the earth.

And these are the generations from Noah to Abram.

Shem, Arphaxad, Salah, Eber, Peleg, Reu, Serug, Nahor, Terah, Abram.

CONVERSATION V.

Mamma.—When Noah left the ark, in what manner did he endeavour to show his gratitude to God for having preserved himself and his family alive?

Esther.—He built an altar and offered burnt offerings thereon.

Mamma.—After Noah had left the ark, what promise did God make to him?

Esther.—God promised that He would no more destroy the earth for man's sake.

Mamma.—What did God tell Noah should be a sign that He would remember His promise?

Esther.—The rainbow.

Mamma.—In what manner do we, in the present day, remember and thank God for this promise?

Ada.—You mean, Mamma, the blessing which we say whenever a rainbow is visible.

Mamma.—Yes, my dear; can you repeat this blessing in Hebrew and in English?

Ada.—בָּרוּךְ אַתָּה יְיָ אֱלֹהֵינוּ מֶלֶךְ הָעוֹלָם זוֹכֵר הַבְּרִית נֶאֱמָן בִּבְרִיתוֹ וְקַיָּם בְּמַאֲמָרוֹ:

Blessed art Thou, O Lord our God, King of the Universe, who remembereth the covenant; is faithful to His covenant, and firm in His promise.

Mamma.—What did God give to Noah and his descendants for food?

Ada.—God gave them permission to eat of the flesh of the animals. Do you think, Mamma, that men had not eaten of the flesh of animals before the flood?

Mamma.—It is probable that they had not, for God only gave Adam and Eve the herbs—that is, vegetables and fruit for food. And we are expressly told that God gave permission to Noah and his family to eat of the flesh of the animals. God also placed a restriction upon this permission;—do you remember what this was?

Ada.—Yes, Noah was forbidden to eat the blood of the animals with the flesh. How do we fulfil this command, Mamma?

Mamma.—After the animals we use for food have been killed so that the blood flows freely according to the command—" Thou shalt pour it upon the ground as water"—a little further preparation is considered necessary by our Rabbis. Have you not noticed that our meat is put in water for half-an-hour, then in salt for an hour, and afterwards well washed in clean water before we attempt to cook it?

Ada.—I have seen the meat in water and in salt, but did not know that it remained in either for any fixed time, neither had I thought of the reason. You spoke just now of our Rabbis, dear Mamma; I thought Moses was the only lawgiver whose laws we considered as binding?

Mamma.—You are right, my dear child, in so far that we should be wrong in following the precepts of any teacher if they were opposed to those laws given us by Moses. When we consider ourselves bound by the precepts of our Rabbis or teachers, it is because they were wise men who devoted their time to the study of God's law, and have considered the best way of fulfilling the commands which God gave us through Moses.

Esther.—But, dear Mamma, can we not read the Bible for ourselves? Are we not told in it everything we ought to do?

Mamma.—In the Bible we are given direct commands, but we are not always told how to fulfil them; we can have no better instance of this than the command we have just been discussing. God told Noah not to eat the blood of the animal; but we find no further particulars as to the method of killing or preparing the meat. If we each read for ourselves, some might think they did sufficient if they did not actually mix the blood with their food; others might think that even the juices of the meat should be extracted, and as many laws will bear different readings, it is necessary to have for our guidance fixed rules. And these rules have been made by pious men who studied from time to time.

Esther.—Do you mean to say, Mamma, that the Rabbis can never be wrong?

Mamma.—Certainly not, my dear child. All human beings are liable to err. All I would wish to impress upon your mind is, never to forsake any observance that you have been taught to conform to, unless you find it is one which contradicts the spirit of our Holy Law. If, as you grow older, there are some observances which appear irksome to you, or you *think* unnecessary, pray do not neglect them until you have taken time to consider, and are *thoroughly convinced* that there is nothing in the Bible to sanction them.

Esther.—Do you think any of our observances irksome, dear Mamma?

Mamma.—I do not think of any that I consider so—but everyone does not think as I do.

Ada and Esther.—I hope we shall always think as you do, dear Mamma.

Mamma.—My dear children, we are chattering and we have not quite finished our questions on this chapter. When Noah's descendants had become numerous, what did they propose to do?

Esther.—To build a city and a tower, whose top should reach to heaven.

Mamma.—For what purpose did they wish to build the tower so high?

Ada.—To make themselves a name, and to prevent themselves from being scattered over the face of the earth.

Mamma.—In what manner was their design frustrated?

Esther.—God confounded their language so that the people could not understand each other.

Mamma.—Can you tell me what the place was called, and the meaning of the word?

Ada.—Yes, it was called Babel, which means confusion.

Mamma.—Name the generations from Noah to Abram.

Ada.—Shem, Arphaxad, Salah, Eber, Peleg, Reu, Serug, Nahor, Terah, Abram.

READING VI.

———o———

Of the race of Shem was Terah, the father of Abram, and the uncle of Lot.

Now God said unto Abram, Get thee out of thy country, Ur of the Chaldees, and from thy kindred, and from thy father's house, unto a land that I will shew thee.

And I will make of thee a great nation, and I will bless thee, and make thy name great; and thou shalt be a blessing: and I will bless them that bless thee, and curse them that curse thee, and in thee shall all the people of the earth be blessed.

And Abram went, as the Lord had spoken unto him; and Lot went with him, for Haran, Abram's brother (the father of Lot), had died in the land of his birth.

And Abram was seventy and five years old when he went out of Haran, where they had dwelt after they left Ur, and where Terah died, whose days were two hundred and five years.

Abram had taken Sarai to wife, but she had no child.

And Abram took Sarai his wife, and Lot his nephew, and all their substance, and all the souls which they had gotten in Haran; and they went forth to go into the land of Canaan; and into the land of Canaan they came.

And Abram passed through the land into the place of Sichem, unto the plain of Moreh.

And God appeared to Abram, and said, Unto thy

seed will I give this land: and Abram builded an altar there unto the Lord.

And Abram went from thence unto a mountain on the east of Bethel, and pitched his tent, having Bethel on the west, and Hai on the east; and there he builded an altar unto the Lord. And he called on the name of the Lord.

And Abram went on toward the south.

Abram went into Egypt to sojourn there; for there was a grievous famine in the land where he dwelt.

And it came to pass, when Abram was come near to enter into Egypt, that he said unto Sarai his wife, Behold now, I know that thou art a fair woman to look upon; therefore it shall come to pass, that when the men of Egypt shall see thee, that they will say, She is his wife, and they will kill me, but they will save thee alive.

Say, I pray thee, thou art my sister; that it may be well with me for thy sake; and my life be saved because of thee.

And it came to pass, when Abram was come into Egypt, that the princes of Pharaoh saw Sarai, and beheld that she was very fair; and they praised her before Pharaoh, and she was taken into his house.

And he treated Abram well for her sake; and he had sheep, and oxen, and asses, and camels, and servants.

And God plagued Pharaoh, because of Sarai, Abram's wife.

And Pharaoh called Abram, and said, What is this that thou hast done? why didst thou not tell me that she was thy wife? I might have taken her to be my wife. Now, therefore, take her, and go thy way.

And they sent Abram away, and his wife, and all that he had.

And Abram went up out of Egypt, he, and his

wife, and all that he had, and Lot with him, into the south.

And Abram was very rich in cattle, and silver, and in gold.

And he went on his journey from the south, even to Bethel, unto the place where his tent had been, and where he had built an altar unto the Lord, between Bethel and Hai; and there Abram called upon the name of the Lord.

And Lot also, who went with Abram, had flocks, and herds, and tents.

And the land was not able to bear them; their substance was so great, that they could not dwell together.

And there was strife between the herdsmen of Abram's cattle, and the herdsmen of Lot's cattle.

And Abram said unto Lot, Let there be no strife, I pray thee, between me and thee, for we are brethren.

Is not the whole land before thee? Remove thyself, I pray thee, from me. If thou wilt take the left hand, then I will go to the right; if thou depart to the right hand, then I will go to the left.

Then Lot chose him all the plain of Jordan eastward, for it was well watered and fertile.

And Abram dwelt in the land of Canaan, and Lot dwelt in the cities of the plain, and pitched his tent towards Sodom.

But the men of Sodom were very wicked before the Lord.

CONVERSATION VI.

Mamma.—When God appeared to Abram and commanded him to leave Ur of the Chaldees, can you remember the words in which this command was given?

Ada.—God said, "Get thee out of thy country, Ur of the Chaldees, and from thy kindred, and from thy father's house, unto a land that I will shew thee."

Mamma.—Do you remember the promise God made Abram at this time?

Ada.—Yes, God said, "I will make of thee a great nation, and I will bless thee, and make thy name great; and thou shalt be a blessing: and I will bless them that bless thee, and curse them that curse thee, and in thee shall all the people of the earth be blessed."

Mamma.—Do you understand the meaning of these words?

Ada.—Not quite, dear Mamma; I do not understand how all the nations of the earth could be blessed through Abram.

Mamma.—When I have explained this, I think you will not find it difficult to understand; but we must, in order to do so, anticipate our history. You are aware that Abram was the father of our own nation—that is, the Jewish or Israelitish nation; so when we read, through Abram, we understand through his descendants. Now, to our nation the law was first given. This law contains all the precepts of morality which are to this day acknowledged by the whole civilised world : wherever these precepts are not acknowledged, men cannot dwell together in peace and safety: thus through us the whole world is blessed.

Ada.—Ought we then to try to make all our neighbours Jews?

Mamma.—By no means: God has never told us that the

Jewish form of worship was the only one acceptable to Him; Jews have never believed this. Our Rabbis teach us that the righteous of all nations are equally acceptable to God, or, figuratively speaking, "*Have a seat in the kingdom of Heaven.*"

Esther.—Then, Mamma, why are we glad that we are born Jews?

Mamma.—I will answer your question by another. If I were to permit you to do anything for me, would you not be delighted with the privilege?

Esther.—Certainly, dear Mamma; if you trust me to go over your cupboards, or your wardrobe, I am always pleased; but I do not see what this has to do with the question.

Mamma.—Then listen attentively, and I think you will understand. We—that is, the Jewish nation—have been chosen by God to confer His blessing upon mankind by preserving, in its purity, the law which He gave through Moses to our forefathers, and by showing to the world at large, through our example, that this law is one to make men good, honest and useful. Is not this a great privilege?

Ada.—It is indeed, dear Mamma; but Jews are not always better than their neighbours.

Mamma.—I am sorry to say we do not always fulfil the precepts of the beautiful law which God has given us; if we did, we must be as good as it is possible for human beings to become. I think now you understand the blessing given to Abram.

Ada and Esther.—Yes, dear Mamma, and we will try to learn and to perform all the Bible teaches us, or we shall not be worthy of the great name we bear.

Mamma.—I pray God, my darlings, you may always have strength to do what is right. Now let us have a few more questions and answers upon the history of Abram that we have been reading about. Who accompanied Abram upon his journey?

Esther.—Sarai his wife, and Lot his nephew.

Mamma.—Why was Lot with Abram?

Esther.—Because Haran, his father, Abram's brother, had died in the land of his birth.

Mamma.—To what place did Abram first journey?

Ada.—To Sichem, in the land of Canaan.

Mamma.—What promise did God make to Abram at Sichem?

Esther.—That He would give the land of Canaan to Abram's descendants.

Mamma.—What caused Abram to leave Canaan and go into Egypt?

Esther.—There was a famine in the land of Canaan.

Mamma.—When Abram came into Egypt, what did he request of Sarai?

Ada.—He desired Sarai to say she was his sister, for he feared lest the men of the place should kill him for her sake.

Esther.—Was it not very wrong of Abram to ask his wife to tell an untruth?

Mamma.—It was wrong, and if you reflect you will perceive that Abram suffered severely on account of it, for Sarai was separated from him in consequence.

Esther.—Then Abram was not always a good man?

Mamma.—Do not say that, my darling; Abram did some things that were wrong. We must not excuse any incorrect action; it is easy for us to know whether the act in itself is right or wrong, but it is not for mortals to judge their fellow men. God alone knows whether the person is good or bad, as He alone can know the thoughts and motives that influence their actions.

Esther.—Then, Mamma, if I know anyone does wrong, I must not say he is wicked.

Mamma.—Certainly not; but you must be careful not to do the same thing: it would be decidedly wicked of you, for you would be aware that you were doing wrong. Now tell me, why did Abram and Lot separate?

Esther.—Because there was not sufficient food for their cattle, and the herdsmen quarrelled.

Mamma.—Have you noticed how generously Abram acted towards Lot? Do you remember his words to Lot upon this occasion?

Ada.—He said, "Let there be no strife between us, for we are brethren. Is not the whole land before thee?

Remove thyself, I pray thee, from me. If thou wilt take the left, I will take the right; if thou depart to the right, then I will go to the left."

Mamma.—What part of the country did Lot choose?

Esther.—The plain of Jordan, for it was well watered and fertile.

Mamma.—What cities were near this plain?

Esther.—Sodom and Gomorrah.

Mamma.—What is remarked of the inhabitants of these cities?

Esther.—That they were very wicked.

READING VII.

ABRAM dwelt in the land of Canaan.

And God said unto Abram, Lift up now thine eyes, and look from the place where thou art, northward and southward, and eastward and westward; for all the land which thou seest, to thee will I give it, and to thy seed for ever.

And I will make thy seed as the dust of the earth.

Arise, walk through the land in the length and in the breadth of it, for to thee will I give it.

Then Abram removed his tent, and came and dwelt in the plain of Mamre, which is in Hebron, and built there an altar unto the Lord.

And it came to pass that many kings of the lands made war, and they took all the goods of Sodom and Gomorrah, and all their victuals.

And they took Lot and his goods, and went their way.

And there came one who had escaped and told Abram.

And when Abram heard that Lot was taken captive, he armed his trained servants, born in his house, three hundred and eighteen, and pursued them unto Dan; and brought back Lot and his goods, and the women and the people.

And the King of Sodom went out to meet Abram on his return from the slaughter.

And the King of Salem brought forth bread and wine; he was a priest of the Most High God.

And the King of Salem blessed Abram and said, Blessed be Abram of the Most High God, possessor of heaven and earth, and blessed be the Most High God, who hath given thine enemies into thy hand. And he gave him tithes of all.

And the King of Sodom said unto Abram, Give me the persons, and take the goods to thyself.

And Abram said to the King of Sodom, I have lift up mine hand unto the Lord, the Most High God, possessor of heaven and earth, that I will not take anything that is thine, lest thou shouldst say I have made Abram rich:

Save only that which the young men have taken, and the portion of the men which went with me, let them take.

After these things the word of the Lord came unto Abram in a vision, saying,

Fear not, Abram, I am thy shield, thy exceeding great reward.

And Abram said, Lord God, what wilt thou give me, seeing I go childless, and lo! one born in my house is my heir.

And behold, the word of the Lord came unto him, saying, This shall not be thine heir; but he that shall be thine heir shall be thine own son.

And God brought Abram forth abroad, and said unto him, Look now towards heaven, and tell the stars if thou be able to number them.

And God said unto Abram, So shall thy seed be.

And Abram believed in the Lord, and God counted it to him for righteousness.

And God said unto Abram, I am the Lord that brought thee out of Ur of the Chaldees, to give thee this land to inherit it.

And Abram said, Lord God, whereby shall I know that I shall inherit it?

And God said unto him, Take a heifer of three

years old, and a she-goat of three years old, and a turtle dove, and a ram of three years old, and a young pigeon.

And he took unto him all these, and parted them in the midst, and laid each piece one against another, but the birds parted he not. And when the fowls came down upon the carcases, Abram drove them away.

And when the sun was going down, a deep sleep fell upon Abram, and lo! a horror, dark and great, fell upon him.

And the Lord said unto Abram, Know of a surety that thy seed shall be strangers in a land that is not theirs, and they shall serve and be afflicted our hundred years.

And also, that nation whom they shall serve, will I judge; and afterwards shall they come out with great substance.

And thou shalt go to thy fathers in peace; thou shalt be buried in a good old age.

But after four hundred years they shall come hither again.

And it came to pass that when the sun went down, and it was dark, behold a smoking furnace, and a burning lamp that passed between those pieces

In the same day the Lord made a covenant with Abram, saying, Unto thy seed have I given this land, from the river of Egypt unto the great river, the river Euphrates.

CONVERSATION VII.

Mamma.—After Abram had separated from Lot, what promise did God make to him?

Ada.—God promised that Abram's descendants should inherit the land of Canaan, and that they should be as numerous as the dust of the earth.

Mamma.—What caused Abram to arm his servants, and to pursue the kings who had made war upon Sodom?

Esther.—Lot, Abram's nephew, had been taken prisoner.

Mamma.—Did Abram accept a portion of the spoil offered to him by the King of Sodom?

Ada.—No; he refused it, saying, "I will not take anything that is thine, lest thou shouldst say, I have made Abram rich."

Esther.—But why, dear Mamma, do you think Abram so particularly objected that the King of Sodom should say he had made Abram rich?

Mamma.—I think that Abram wished to show the King of Sodom that he accepted the increase of his riches as a blessing from God, and that he did not wish to feel himself indebted to man. Also, that he had made war with no idea of profit to himself; and that it was only right to do so in defence of one's self, or one's kindred. Do you remember how God signified His approval of Abram's conduct in this affair?

Ada.—Yes; God appeared to him in a vision, saying, "Fear not, Abram, I am thy shield, and thy exceeding great reward."

Mamma.—What promise did God make to Abram at this time?

Esther.—That he should have a son.

Mamma.—When Abram fell asleep at the setting of the sun, what were the words he heard in his vision?

Ada.—He heard God say, "Know of a surety that thy seed shall be strangers in a land that is not theirs, and they shall serve them, and they shall afflict them four hundred years."

Mamma.—After Abram's descendants had been in this strange land four hundred years, what did God promise to do to this nation?

Ada.—God promised that He would judge this nation, and that Abram's descendants should come forth with great substance.

Mamma.—This prophecy was fulfilled by the sojourning of the children of Israel in Egypt, and their subsequent redemption. What district of the country was promised to Abram for his descendants?

Ada.—The country lying between the river of Egypt and the Euphrates.

READING VIII.

―――o―――

AFTER Abram had dwelt ten years in Canaan, and Sarai had no child, Sarai gave her handmaid, Hagar, an Egyptian, to Abram to wife, that he might obtain children by her.

But when Hagar knew that she should have a child, her mistress was despised in her eyes.

And Sarai told Abram, and said, The Lord judge between me and thee. And Abram said to Sarai, Behold, thy maid is in thy hand; do to her as it pleaseth thee. And when Sarai dealt hardly with her, she fled from her face.

And the angel of the Lord found her by a spring, in the way of Shur. And he said, Hagar, Sarai's maid, whence comest thou? and whither wilt thou go? And she said, I flee from the face of my mistress, Sarai.

And the angel of the Lord said unto her, Return unto thy mistress, and submit thyself unto her hands, and I will multiply thy seed greatly, that it shall not be numbered for multitude. Thou shalt have a son, and his name shall be called Ishmael; because the Lord hath heard thy affliction. And he will be a wild man; his hand will be against every man, and every man's hand against him; and he shall dwell in the presence of all his brethren.

And Hagar said, Thou God seest me. And Hagar bare Abram a son, and he called his name Ishmael.

When Abram was ninety and nine years old, God appeared unto him, and said, I am the Almighty God; walk before Me, and be thou perfect. And I will make My covenant between Me and thee, and will multiply thee greatly.

And Abram fell on his face, and God spake to him, saying, I am the Almighty. Behold, My covenant is with thee; thou shalt become a father of many nations.

Thy name shall no more be called Abram, but thy name shall be called Abraham; for a father of many nations will I make thee, and my covenant shall be with thee and with thy seed after thee for an everlasting covenant.

This is my covenant. Every male child among you shall be circumcised, and if he be not circumcised that soul shall be cut off from among his people.

And Sarai, thy wife, thou shalt no longer call Sarai; her name shall be Sarah. And I will bless her, and give her also a son, and she shall be the mother of nations.

Then Abraham fell on his face, and laughed; therefore was his son's name called Isaac. And God said, I will establish my covenant with Isaac, and with his seed after him.

And Abraham said unto God, O that Ishmael might live before thee! And God said, As for Ishmael, I have heard thee; behold, I have blessed him.

And Abraham was ninety and nine years old when he entered into the covenant, and Ishmael was thirteen years old.

And the Lord appeared unto Abraham, in the plains of Mamre, as he sat in the tent door in the heat of the day: and he lifted up his eyes and looked, and lo, three men stood by him; and when he saw them, he ran to meet them from the tent door, and bowed himself towards the ground, and said:

My Lord, if now I have found favour in thy sight, pass not away, I pray thee, from thy servant; let a little water, I pray you, be fetched, and wash your feet, and rest yourselves under the tree; and I will fetch a morsel of bread, and comfort ye your hearts. After that ye shall pass on, since ye have once passed by your servant.

And they said, So do, as thou hast said. And Abraham hastened into the tent unto Sarah, and said, Make ready three measures of fine meal, knead it, and make cakes upon the hearth. And Abraham ran unto the herd, and fetched a calf tender and good, and gave it unto a young man to dress it. And he took butter and milk, and the calf which he had dressed, and set it before them; and he stood by them under the tree, and they did eat.

And they said, Where is Sarah, thy wife? And Abraham said, Behold, in the tent. And the angel said, Lo Sarah thy wife, shall have a son. And Sarah heard it in the tent door, which was behind him, and she laughed within herself.

And he said unto Abraham, Wherefore did Sarah laugh, saying, Shall I of a surety have a child who am old? Is any thing too hard for the Lord? I will return unto thee according to the time of life, and Sarah shall have a son.

And the men rose up thence, and looked towards Sodom; and Abraham went to bring them on their way.

CONVERSATION VIII.

Mamma.—When Hagar had, at Sarai's request, become Abraham's wife, and knew that she would have a child, how did she behave to Sarai?

Esther.—She despised her.

Mamma.—When Sarai complained to Abram of Hagar's conduct, what did he say?

Ada.—He said, "Behold, thy maid is in thy hand; do to her as it pleaseth thee."

Mamma.—When Sarai dealt hardly with Hagar, what happened?

Esther.—Hagar fled into the wilderness. There an angel of God addressed her, and told her to return, and submit herself to her mistress.

Mamma.—Did the angel say anything further to Hagar?

Ada.—Yes, he told her she should have a son, and that his name should be called Ishmael, which means "God heareth," for God had heard her affliction.

Mamma.—Can you remember how God addressed Abram after the birth of Ishmael?

Ada.—God appeared to Abram, and said, "I am the Almighty God אל שׁדי (El Shadday); walk before me, and be thou perfect."

Mamma.—At this time God changed Abram's name and the name of his wife Sarai; can you remember the signification of Abraham and the promise given at the same time?

Ada.—Abraham means father of many nations; and God promised at this time that Sarah should have a son.

Mamma.—Why was this son to be called Isaac?

Esther.—Because when Abraham was told that Sarah should have a son, he rejoiced and laughed.

Mamma.—You understand, then, that Isaac means laughter. What was Abraham's prayer for Ishmael?

Ada.—He said, "O that Ishmael might live before Thee?"

Esther.—What does this mean, Mamma? Did Abraham think that Ishmael would die?

Mamma.—We do not understand by the words of Abraham's prayer that he feared any immediate danger for Ishmael, but that he prayed that Ishmael might prosper in God's presence, and do what was right in His sight.

Esther.—Did God grant Abraham's prayer?

Mamma.—Yes, God told Abraham that He would bless Ishmael, and that he should become the father of nations. From Ishmael are descended many of the Arab tribes, and most of the Mahometans, which nations believe in "One God" only, and are forbidden by their laws to worship idols.

Esther.—When Abraham saw the three men he does not appear to have known that they were angels.

Mamma.—You are right, my dear; he took them for travellers, and treated them as such, with that courtesy and hospitality which was the custom of the country in which he lived.

Esther.—It seems very strange that Abraham should have brought the angels water to wash their feet.

Mamma.—You will not think it strange when you learn that, in ancient days, and even in the present day, in the East (where Abraham dwelt), people did not wear shoes and stockings, but sandals. The roads being hot and sandy, washing the feet was a very necessary refreshment.

Esther.—What are angels, dear Mamma? The angels that appeared to Abraham could not have had wings like those I see in your picture Bible, or Abraham must have known that they were not men?

Mamma.—I am glad to find that you think carefully over our readings, although you have asked me a somewhat difficult question. I cannot undertake to tell you what angels really are; they may be some class of beings superior to man; the same Creator who formed men can form whatsoever He pleases. All that it concerns us to know is, that whatever may be the nature of angels, they are entirely subservient to the will of the Almighty. The word מַלְאָךְ (Mol-och) angel means simply messenger, and may even be applied to a human being, sent on a mission from the Almighty. I must caution you, my dear child, to form no ideas from the pictures you see in Bibles edited by persons who are not of our faith; most of the plates are taken from the paintings of Catholics, or even Heathens, who entertain very different ideas from our own.

Ada.—We read that Abraham brought butter and milk with the meat which he set before the angels,—was not this wrong?

Mamma.—There are many customs observed at the present day, which were unknown to Abraham. The law was not given until four hundred years after this time, therefore he could not be said to transgress it. Tell me, Esther, what was the angel's mission to Abraham?

Esther.—They told Abraham that Sarah his wife should have a son.

Mamma.—When Sarah laughed, thinking it improbable, after having been so many years without children, she should now have a son, what did the angel say?

Esther.—He said, " Is anything too hard for the Lord?"

READING IX.

———o———

AND God said, shall I hide from Abraham that thing which I am about to do, seeing that Abraham shall become a great and mighty nation, and all the nations of the earth shall be blessed in him!

For I know him, that he will command his children, and his household after him. And they shall keep the way of the Lord, to do righteousness and justice in order that the Lord may bring upon Abraham that which He hath spoken of him.

And the Lord said, Because the sins of Sodom and Gomorrah are very great, I will go down now, and see whether they have done like to the cry of it, which has come up before me.

And the men turned their faces from there, and went towards Sodom. But Abraham stood yet before the Lord.

And he drew near and said, Wilt thou destroy the righteous with the wicked? That be far from thee. If there be fifty righteous within the city, wilt thou not spare the place for the fifty righteous that may be therein? Will not the judge of all the earth do right?

And the Lord said, If I find fifty righteous within the city, then will I spare all the place for their sakes.

And Abraham said, Behold now, I have taken upon me to speak unto the Lord, who am but dust and ashes: if there lack five of the fifty righteous wilt thou destroy all the city for lack of five? And God said, If I find forty and five, I will not destroy it.

And Abraham spake again, and said, If there shall be forty found there? And God said, I will not destroy it for forty's sake.

And Abraham said, Oh, let not the Lord be angry, and I will speak; if there should be thirty found? And God said, I will not do it for thirty's sake.

And Abraham said, Behold, now, I have taken upon me to speak unto the Lord: if there shall be twenty found? And God said, I will not destroy it for twenty's sake.

And Abraham said, Oh let not the Lord be angry, and I will speak but this once: if ten shall be found there? And God said, If ten shall be found there I will not destroy it, for ten's sake. And the Lord went his way; and Abraham returned unto his own place.

And there came two angels at even to Sodom; and Lot sat in the gate, and seeing them, rose up to meet them; and bowed himself with his face towards the ground. And said, Behold now, my lords, turn in, I pray you, into your servant's house, and wash your feet, and tarry all night, and ye shall rise up early, and go your ways.

And they turned in; and he made a feast, and they did eat. And they said unto Lot, Hast thou any here besides thy sons and thy daughters? Whatsoever thou hast in this place, bring them out, for we will destroy it, because the cry of them has waxen great before the Lord, who has sent us to destroy it.

And Lot went out, and spake unto the men who had married his daughters, and said, Up, get ye out of this place; for the Lord will destroy this city; but he seemed as one that mocked unto them.

And when the morning arose the men said, Arise, take thy wife and thy daughters which are here, lest thou be consumed. And while he lingered, the men laid hold upon his hand, and upon the hand of his two daughters, the Lord being merciful unto him.

And they brought him forth, and set him without the city, and said, Escape for thy life, look not behind thee, neither stay thou in all the plain; escape to the mountains, lest thou be consumed.

And Lot said, Oh, not so, my Lord, behold now, this city is near, to flee unto, and it is a little one. Oh, let me escape thither (is it not a little one?) and my soul shall live.

And he said unto Lot, See, I have accepted thee in this thing also; I will not destroy this city, for which thou hast spoken. Haste thee, escape thither, for I cannot do anything till thou be come thither. Therefore the name of the city was called Zoar.

Then God rained upon Sodom and Gomorrah brimstone and fire out of heaven, and overthrew those cities of the plain, and all the people, and that which grew upon the ground.

But Lot's wife looked back, and she became a pillar of salt.

And Abraham got up early in the morning to the place where he stood before the Lord; and he looked toward Sodom and Gomorrah, and toward all the land of the plain, and lo! the smoke of the country went up as the smoke of a furnace.

And Lot went up, and dwelt in the mountains, and his two daughters with him.

CONVERSATION IX.

Mamma.—Do you remember why God said that He would make known to Abraham the judgment He was about to bring upon Sodom and Gomorrah?

Ada.—Because Abraham was to become a great and mighty nation, and all the nations of the earth were to be blessed through him.

Mamma.—In this instance God gives us His reason for having thus favored Abraham. Can you repeat the words of the text?

Ada.—God said of Abraham, "For I know him that he will command his children, and his household after him. And they shall keep the way of the Lord to do righteousness and justice."

Esther.—Does it not appear presumptuous of Abraham that he should have renewed his prayer so often, after God had promised to grant what he asked?

Mamma.—It is natural to think so on first reading this history; but we find that God was not displeased with Abraham. Therefore we are led to consider the lesson which this chapter is intended to convey to us, namely, that God approves of men being merciful towards their fellow creatures, and that we should not rejoice in the punishment of sinners. We are also shown the great mercy of God, for had there been but ten righteous people in the cities, God would have saved the whole for the sake of the ten.

Ada.—Do you think, Mamma, that Abraham endeavoured to teach the people of Sodom and Gomorrah, and tried to make them any better.

Mamma.—It appears to me, my dear, that he did all that was in his power. When he refused presents from the Sodomites after the rescue of Lot and their own people, it was doubtless with the view of showing them strict justice, and trust in God. It is only by example that we can hope to influence others; we cannot force upon them our religious convictions.

Ada.—Do you think, then, that we ought not to try to teach other nations our own religion?

Mamma.—I think we ought to endeavour to bring all nations to acknowledge the "one true God," but this must not be done by trying to convert them to our religion; our chief aim should be, to make ourselves worthy of the blessing of Abraham by shewing to other nations that it is to the Jew they must look for examples of justice, judgment, mercy, and proper teaching of the laws of God to their children and their households.

Ada.—I do not quite understand how we can shew justice and judgment when we have no longer a country or judges of our own.

Mamma.—You think, then, that there can be no justice or judgment, but of such cases as are brought before a court of law; you have forgotten the many transactions of every day life, the treatment of each other, of our servants, and indeed of every one we may have to deal with, in all the relations of life. We should be more careful of our conduct, and are more to blame than people of other nations if we do not act with the strictest honour.

Esther.—Why, dear Mamma, ought we to be better than other people?

Mamma.—For two reason: firstly, because as the law was given to us we ought to know better than others; secondly, when a Jew acts in the slightest way dishonourably, he brings discredit upon the whole of his nation. Now tell me, Esther, how did Sodom and Gomorrah fall?

Esther.—They were destroyed by brimstone and fire which God rained from heaven upon them.

Mamma.—To what city did Lot make his escape?

Esther.—To Zoar.

Mamma.—What became of Lot's wife?

Ada.—She looked back upon the cities and became a pillar of salt.

Mamma.—We should learn from her fate implicit

obedience to the commands of God. Lot's family were specially enjoined not to look behind them. We do not suppose that Lot's wife was miraculously changed into a pillar of salt, but that the substances that were falling on the city overtook her, and being covered with them, she stood there a pillar of resinous matter. Travellers at the present day find remains of the bituminous substance in the region where these cities are supposed to have stood. The Dead Sea covers a great portion of the land upon which Sodom and Gomorrah, Admar and Zeboim were built. In this sea it is said nothing can live, and birds as they fly over its surface are often killed by the vapours which ascend from it. After the destruction of Sodom and Gomorrah we hear no more of Lot, but we are told that the Ammonites and Moabites (so frequently mentioned in the Scripture History), are descended from his daughters.

READING X.

And Abraham went toward the south country, and dwelt between Kadesh and Shur, and abode for a time in Gerar.

And the Lord visited Sarah as He had spoken, and she bare Abraham a son in his old age, at the set time of which God had said. And Abraham called the name of his son, whom Sarah bare to him, Isaac.

And Abraham was one hundred years old when his son was born. And the child grew, and was weaned. And Abraham made a great feast on the day that Isaac was weaned.

And Sarah saw the son of Hagar mocking, wherefore she said unto Abraham, Cast out this bondwoman and her son; for the son of the bondwoman shall not be heir with my son, even with Isaac. And the thing was very grievous in Abraham's sight, because of the lad.

And God said unto Abraham, Let it not grieve thee, because of the lad, and because of thy bondwoman; in all that Sarah hath said unto thee do; for in Isaac shall thy seed be called.

And also of the son of the bondwoman will I make a great nation, because he is thy seed.

And Abraham rose up early in the morning, and took bread, and a bottle of water, and gave it unto Hagar, and sent them away. And they departed into the wilderness of Beersheba.

And the water was spent in the bottle, and she cast her son under one of the shrubs, and went and sat down over against him a good way off, as it were a bowshot; for she said, Let me not see the death of the child. And she lift up her voice and wept.

And God heard the voice of the lad; and the angel of God called to Hagar out of heaven, and said unto her, What aileth thee, Hagar? fear not; for God hath heard the voice of the lad where he is arise, and lift him up, and hold him in thine hand, for I will make of him a great nation.

And God opened her eyes, and she saw a well of water; and she went and filled the bottle with water, and gave the lad to drink.

And God was with him, and he grew and dwelt in the wilderness of Paran, and became a great archer; and his mother took him a wife out of the land of Egypt.

CONVERSATION X.

Mamma.—Where did Lot and his daughters dwell after the destruction of Sodom and Gomorrah?

Esther.—They dwelt in the mountains.

Mamma.—Did Abraham remove?

Esther.—Yes, and dwelt for a time in Gerar.

Mamma.—How old was Abraham when his son Isaac was born?

Esther.—He was one hundred years old.

Mamma.—Why were Hagar and Ishmael sent away?

Esther.—Because Sarah saw Ishmael mocking Isaac.

Ada.—Does it not appear very unkind of Abraham to allow them to be sent away from their home?

Mamma.—It certainly does appear so when we first read this chapter, but if you consider the subject, you will find that God told Abraham to listen to Sarah's voice; therefore it must have been right that they should go. We are apt to fancy Ishmael a little child, while in fact he was more than thirteen years of age. We may learn from this history that, if brothers cannot agree well together, it is better that they should be separated than that an ill feeling should grow up between them. You will find that when Isaac and Ishmael had both grown to manhood they must have been on friendly terms, for after Abraham's death their names are mentioned together as having buried their father.

Esther.—How was it, dear Mamma, that Hagar thought that Ishmael would die when they had drunk all the water?

Mamma.—Because, my dear, in a hot country such as they were travelling in, thirst becomes absolutely painful and dangerous. You are quite right to ask any question, and try to ascertain the reason of anything that may appear strange to you in our Bible history, but you must not expect always to receive answers that you can understand at present. The events of our history took place in a country very different from the one we live in; therefore to understand many of our customs, it is necessary to learn a great deal more of the land of Canaan and the surrounding countries than I can undertake to teach you in our simple conversations. When you are older, you will be able to read for yourself the accounts of travellers that will interest you. Now, tell me what became of Ishmael in the words of the text, if you remember them?

Esther.—" God was with him, and he grew and dwelt in the wilderness of Paran, and became a great archer; and his mother took him a wife out of the land of Egypt."

Mamma.—What do you understand by the words " God was with him?"

Ada.—That God protected him.

READING XI.

———o———

AND it came to pass about this time that Abimelech and Phichol, his captain, spake to Abraham, saying, God is with thee in all that thou doest.

Now, therefore, swear unto me that thou wilt not deal falsely with me nor with my children after me, but that thou wilt do unto me according to the kindness I have done unto thee.

Then Abraham said, I will swear. And Abraham reproached Abimelech on account of a well of water which Abimelech's servants had violently seized. But Abimelech said, I know not who hath done this thing, nor have I heard of it until to-day.

Then Abraham took sheep and oxen and gave them unto Abimelech, and both of them made a covenant.

And Abraham set seven ewe lambs by themselves, and Abimelech said, What mean these seven ewe lambs?

Then Abraham said, It is that thou shalt take them of me as a witness that I have digged this well. Therefore Abraham called the place Beersheba, because there both of them sware.

And Abimelech and Phichol returned into the land of the Philistines.

And Abraham planted a grove and called on the name of the Lord, the everlasting God. And Abraham sojourned in the land of the Philistines many days.

And it came to pass, after these things, that God

tried Abraham, and said unto him, Abraham! And he said, Behold, here I am.

And God said, Take now thy son, thine only son Isaac, whom thou lovest, and get thee into the land of Moriah, and offer him there for a burnt offering, upon one of the mountains, which I will tell thee of.

And Abraham rose up early in the morning, and saddled his ass, and took two of his young men with him, and Isaac his son, and clave the wood for a burnt offering, and went unto the place of which God had told him.

Then, on the third day, Abraham lifted up his eyes, and saw the place afar off. And he said unto the men, Abide you here with the ass, and I and the lad will go yonder, and worship, and come again to you.

And Abraham took the wood of the burnt offering, and laid it upon his son Isaac; and he took the fire in his hand and a knife; and they went together.

And Isaac said, My father. And Abraham answered, Here am I, my son. And Isaac said, Here is the fire and the wood, but where is the lamb for a burnt offering?

And Abraham said, My son, God will provide Himself a lamb for a burnt offering. So they went on together.

And they came to the place which God had told him of; and he built an altar there, and laid the wood in order, and bound Isaac his son, and laid him upon the altar on the wood. And Abraham stretched forth his hand to slay his son.

And the angel of the Lord called unto him out of heaven, and said, Abraham! Abraham! And he said, Here am I. And he said, Lay not thine hand upon the lad, neither do thou any thing unto him, for now I know that thou fearest God, seeing thou hast not withheld thine only son from me.

And Abraham lifted up his eyes, and looked, and behold behind him a ram caught in a thicket by his horns. And Abraham went, and took the ram, and offered him up for a burnt offering, instead of his son. And Abraham called the name of that place Adonai Jireh.

And the angel of the Lord called unto Abraham the second time, saying—

By myself have I sworn, saith the Lord, because thou hast done this thing and hast not withheld thy son, thine only son, that in blessing I will bless thee and I will multiply thy seed as the stars of heaven, and as the sand which is upon the sea-shore, and thy seed shall possess the gate of his enemies, and in thy seed shall all the nations of the earth be blessed: because thou hast obeyed my voice.

And Abraham returned unto his young men, and they rose up and went to Beersheba, where Abraham dwelt.

CONVERSATION XI.

Mamma.—Do you remember why Abimelech said that he wished to make a covenant of peace with Abraham?

Ada.—Because he saw that God was with him in all things.

Mamma.—Before Abraham concluded the treaty, on what account did he reproach Abimelech?

Esther.—On account of the well of water which Abimelech's servants had violently taken from Abraham's servants.

Mamma.—What answer did Abimelech make to this charge?

Esther.—He said, "he knew not who had done so, neither had he heard of it at all until this day."

Mamma.—Have you noticed that in the days of Abraham, as in the present days, gifts were considered a sign of goodwill and friendship?

Ada.—Yes; I did remark that Abraham set aside seven ewe lambs which he offered to Abimelech. I have also noticed that most places that are mentioned in the Bible derive their names from circumstances that took place in their vicinity.

Mamma.—I am glad you have remarked this, for if you remember the names of the places, you will through the signification of them, be reminded of the events to which they allude. Tell Esther the name Abraham gave to the well, and its signification?

Ada.—Abraham called the well בְּאֵר־שָׁבַע Beïr Shobang, which means "Well of the oath."

Esther.—May I ask you a question, dear Mamma? I am not sure that it is right to do so, but I should like to know why God told Abraham to offer his son Isaac as a burnt offering? If God knows all our thoughts, as you have often told me He does, He would have known that

Abraham would do as He commanded, and need not have tried him.

Mamma.—My dear child, I never object to any questions you may ask as long as you try to learn.

This is a very natural question, and has occurred to wiser and older minds than yours. I cannot pretend to explain to you all the ways of our Almighty Father; but of this you may rest satisfied, that He is good and just. As regards the trial of Abraham's faith, I think (and I believe some of our teachers who have studied the Bible are of the same opinion) that God tried Abraham in this way, in order to show *us*, how much he would sacrifice at the command of God. For although God certainly must have known what Abraham would do, we should not have had the example, had not this deed been recorded in our Bible.

Esther.—How can Abraham's conduct in this instance be an example for us; we are never likely to be tried in the same way?

Mamma.—Certainly, my dear, we could never be similarly tried, for we know that God would not accept a human sacrifice; but there are many ways in which men may follow Abraham's example. If we give up all prospects of wealth, or worldly advancements, in order to observe the Sabbath or any other of God's laws, we are in part following Abraham's example.

Ada.—Do you mean then, Mamma, that by Abraham's willingness to sacrifice Isaac we should learn to have perfect faith in God, and to know that whatever He commands us is for our good?

Mamma.—Yes, my dear, this is the lesson I think this history is meant to teach us; also, that however our inclination may lead us to act otherwise, we should always endeavour strictly to obey the Law of God, and rest assured that our Almighty Father will never try us beyond our powers of endurance.

Esther and Ada.—We will try to remember this, dear Mamma. Will you not read us a little more to-day?

Mamma.—No, my dear children; I will ask one more question, and then you must go and play Esther, for I have given you quite enough to think about.

Ada.—May I guess your last question, Mamma?

Mamma.—Yes, my dear; and if you are right, you may answer it.

Ada.—You wish us to tell you the name Abraham gave to the place upon which he was to have sacrificed his son. It was יְיָ יִרְאֶה (Adonai Jireh) which means "the Lord will provide," for God had provided a ram to be sacrificed instead of Isaac.

Esther.—The ram that was caught in the thicket by its horns?

Mamma.—Yes, darling. Good-bye, for a little while, we have had talk enough for to-day.

READING XII.

And Sarah was one hundred and seven and twenty years old, and she died in Hebron, in the land of Canaan. And Abraham came to mourn for Sarah and to weep for her.

And Abraham stood up from before his dead, and spake unto the sons of Heth, saying, I am a stranger, and a sojourner with you. Give me a possession of a burying-place with you, that I may bury my dead out of my sight.

And they said unto him, Hear us, my lord: thou art a mighty prince amongst us. In the choice of our sepulchres bury thy dead.

And Abraham stood up and bowed himself to the people of the land, even to the children of Heth, and said, If it be your mind that I should bury my dead out of my sight, hear me, and entreat for me to Ephron, the son of Zoar, that he may give me the cave of Machpelah which he hath, which is in the end of the field: for as much money as it is worth he shall give it me for a burying-place.

And Ephron the Hittite answered Abraham, in the audience of all the people, and said, Nay, my lord, hear me: the field give I thee, and the cave that is therein give I thee: bury thy dead.

But Abraham said, I will give thee money for the field; take it of me, and I will bury my dead there. And after this, Abraham buried Sarah his wife, in the cave which he bought, in the land of Canaan; and which was made sure unto him for a possession.

And when Abraham was very old, and the Lord had blessed him in all things, he said unto his oldest servant, who ruled over all that he had,

Put, I pray thee, thy hand under my thigh, and swear by the God of heaven and earth, that thou wilt not take a wife unto my son of the daughters of the land in which I dwell. But thou shalt go to my country, and to my kindred, and there take a wife unto my son Isaac.

And the servant said unto him, If the woman will not come with me into this land, must I take thy son into the land whence thou camest?

And Abraham said unto him, Beware that thou takest not my son thither again. The Lord God of heaven which took me from my father's house, and from the land of my kindred, and which spake unto me, and which sware unto me, saying, Unto thy seed will I give this land, he shall send his angels before thee; and thou shalt take a wife unto my son from thence.

And if the woman be not willing to follow thee, then thou shalt be clear from this oath, only take not my son thither again.

And the servant put his hand under the thigh of Abraham, his master, and sware concerning that matter.

And the servant took ten camels, and departed, and went into the city of Nahor.

CONVERSATION XII.

Mamma.—How old was Sarah when she died?

Esther.—One hundred and twenty-seven years.

Mamma.—For what purpose did Abraham address the sons of Heth?

Esther.—To ask them to allow him to purchase a burying-place.

Mamma.—Can you name the burying-place Abraham wished to purchase?

Esther.—It was called the cave of Machpelah.

Ada.—Do you think, Mamma, that Abraham had any reason for refusing the cave and the field as a gift, when Ephron the Hittite offered it to him?

Mamma.—Yes, my dear, I think in the first place that Abraham wished to make the possession of his burying-place secure to his descendants by having paid before witnesses the exact value of the cave and field. I also think that the speeches of Ephron the Hittite were in a measure complimentary, and that he had no more idea of making Abraham a present of this land, than we have of performing menial offices for a person to whom we may subscribe ourselves, "Your obedient or humble servant;" but when we have finished our conversation with Esther, I will read you the notes from Kitto's edition of the Bible upon this subject. I think Esther will be tired, for she is rather too young to understand them. Esther will tell me what occurred after the death and burial of Sarah?

Esther.—Abraham called his eldest servant and made him swear, that he would go to Abraham's own country to seek a wife for Isaac.

Mamma.—Why do you think Abraham objected that

Isaac should take a wife from the daughters of the land in which he dwelt?

Ada.—I suppose, Mamma, because the people of Canaan were idolaters, and that Abraham feared they would lead Isaac away from the worship of the true God.

Mamma.—You are right, my dear; thus you see that even before our law was given, it was thought most advisable only to marry those who shared the same religious faith with ourselves.

Ada.—Eleazar does not appear to have been very ready to go upon his errand.

Mamma.—What makes you think that, my dear?

Ada.—Because, before he would take the oath Abraham required of him, he asked what he should do, if the damsel were not willing to accompany him, or if her friends would not let her come.

Mamma.—You have not thought quite sufficiently upon this subject, my dear, or, instead of fancying that Eleazar made any objection to his errand, you would see what a good and faithful servant he was; how strict a regard he had for truth, and how careful he was to make no promise he could not be sure of performing.

Esther.—But he did promise, Mamma.

Mamma.—Yes, when Abraham told him that he felt sure God would grant His protection, that *He* would send His angels before him, and that if he did not succeed, " he should be clear from the oath."

Esther.—For what purpose did Eleazar take ten camels with him to Nahor?

Mamma.—To serve as beasts of burden, to carry him and the presents which he was taking to the relatives of the woman who should be Isaac's wife, and to herself. Camels are still used in the East instead of horses; they are more capable of enduring fatigue, and can exist longer without water. In these countries travellers are obliged to traverse sandy deserts, where sometimes there is no water to be found for some distance.

READING XIII.

―――o―――

And Abraham's servant came to Mesopotamia unto the city of Nahor. And he made his camels to kneel down without the city by a well of water, at the time in the evening when the women go out to draw water.

And he said, O Lord God of my master Abraham, I pray thee, send me good speed this day, and shew kindness unto my master Abraham.

Behold, I stand here by the well, and the women come here to draw water: let it come to pass, that the damsel to whom I shall say, Let down thy pitcher, I pray thee, that I may drink; and she shall say, Drink, and I will give thy camels drink also: let the same be she that thou hast appointed for thy servant Isaac; and thereby shall I know that thou hast shewed kindness unto my master.

And it came to pass before he had done speaking, that behold, Rebekah came out with the pitcher upon her shoulder. And the damsel was very fair.

And she went down to the well, and filled her pitcher; and when she was come up, the servant ran to meet her, and said, Let me, I pray thee, drink a little water out of thy pitcher:

And she said, Drink, my lord: and she hastened to let down her pitcher upon her hand, and gave him drink.

And when he had done drinking, she said, I

will draw water for thy camels also, until they have done drinking. And she hastened, and emptied her pitcher into the trough, and ran again unto the well to draw water, and drew for all his camels.

And the man, wondering at her, held his peace, thinking that the Lord had prospered him.

And when the camels had done drinking, the man took a golden earring, and two bracelets, and gave them to her.

And he said, Whose daughter art thou? And she said, I am the daughter of Bethuel, the son of Milcah, which she bare unto Nahor, Abraham's brother.

And Eleazar said, Tell me, I pray thee, is there room in thy father's house for us to lodge in?

And she said unto him, We have straw and provender enough, and room to lodge in.

And the man bowed down his head, and worshipped the Lord.

And he said, Blessed be the Lord God of my master Abraham, who hast not left him destitute of His mercy and His truth; and hast led me in the way to the house of my master's brethren.

And the damsel ran and told her friends these things.

And Rebekah had a brother whose name was Laban: and he ran out, unto the well, to the man, after he had seen the earring and the bracelets upon his sister, and when he had heard the words which she spake unto him.

And Laban said unto the man, Come in, thou blessed of the Lord; wherefore standest thou without, for the house and the room for the camels are prepared? And the man came into the house.

And Laban ungirded the camels, and gave straw and provender for them, and water was set to wash the man's feet, and the feet of the men who were with him, and there was meat set before them to eat.

But he said, I will not eat until I have told my errand.

And they said, Speak on.

CONVERSATION XIII.

Mamma.—Can you tell me the name of the country to which Abraham's servant journeyed?

Esther.—He journeyed to Mesopotamia, and came to the city of Nahor.

Mamma.—Who was Nahor?

Esther.—Abraham's brother.

Mamma.—What was Eleazar's first act on arriving at the end of his journey?

Ada.—You mean, Mamma, his prayer to God that he might succeed on his errand?

Mamma.—Yes, my dear, have you noticed anything remarkable in the way this prayer was answered?

Esther.—Oh, yes, dear Mamma; it seemed very strange that Rebekah should say the very words Eleazar ha prayed for.

Ada.—Do you not think, Mamma, that Eleazar wished to test the disposition of the woman who was to be his master's son's wife; to find out if she were obliging and good natured.

Mamma.—It is quite possible he may have had some idea of the kind. There is more of Rebekah's disposition shewn in the account we have just read, than we are able to gather from a hasty perusal of the narrative.

Esther.—What do you mean, dear Mamma? We only read that she went down to the well for water, and when the man asked her, she gave him water and drew for his camels also.

Mamma.—Have you noticed that Rebekah went about her duties without loitering on her way? She did not stop to gaze about, and had not noticed the traveller until he accosted her.

Esther.—You mean this as a lesson to me, dear Mamma, that I should not stop to play and look about, when you send me on a message.

Mamma.—My darling, since you are willing to apply the lesson you need not look so sad; I am glad to find you remember your own faults. I had quite forgotten your little neglect of my message yesterday; and since you are so sorry, I feel sure you will not do the same again; so kiss me, darling, and then tell me what Eleazar said to Rebekah after she had drawn water for all his camels?

Esther.—He asked her, Whose daughter she was, and gave her presents of bracelets and an earring.

Mamma.—And who was the father of Rebekah?

Esther.—Bethuel.

Mamma.—And Bethuel was the son of Nahor, Abraham's brother. When Eleazar heard who Rebekah was, what did he next?

Esther.—He asked, if there was room in her father's house for him to lodge in.

Mamma.—You are quite correct, my dear, although you have not given me the answer I was thinking of.

Ada.—I know what you mean, Mamma; you wished us to notice, that Eleazar did not forget to thank God for having granted his prayer.

Mamma.—That is what I meant, and I should like you to repeat the text if you can remember it.

Ada.—The man bowed his head, and worshipped the Lord, and he said, " Blessed be the Lord God of my master Abraham, who hast not left him destitute of His mercy and His truth; and hast led me in the way to the house of my master's brethren."

Mamma.—When Rebekah had told her mother and her brother of the presents Abraham's servant had given her, and made known to them his request, how did Laban act?

Esther.—He ran directly to the man, and said, " Come in, thou blessed of the Lord," and told him that the room was prepared for his camels.

Mamma.—And when they had come in, that is, Eleazar and the men who were with him, and had washed their feet, did Eleazar partake of the food that was set before him?

Esther.—No; he refused to do so, until he had told his errand.

Mamma.—You may learn from this conduct what a good and faithful servant Eleazar was; he would not think of his own refreshment until he had accomplished his master's business.

Ada.—Mamma, dear, you spoke just now of the men who were with Eleazar. We did not read at first that he took men with him.

Mamma.—I am pleased, my dear, that you are so attentive to our readings; your remark is correct, but such omissions do not in the slightest degree impair the truth of our Biblical narrative; we know that many persons must have existed who are not even mentioned in the Bible; such people only are written of as were connected with particular events. The men who went with Eleazar were merely servants, and are therefore only casually mentioned; our own sense would lead us to suppose that ten camels must require more than one man to direct them.

READING XIV.

And Eleazar said, I am Abraham's servant. And the Lord hath blessed my master greatly, and he is become great: and He hath given him flocks, and herds, and silver, and gold, and men-servants, and maid-servants, and camels, and asses.

And Sarah, my master's wife, bare a son unto my master when she was old; and unto him hath he given all that he hath.

And my master made me swear, saying, Thou shalt not take a wife unto my son of the daughters of the land wherein I dwell; but thou shalt go unto my father's house, and to my kindred, and take a wife unto my son.

And I said unto my master, If the woman will not come with me?

And he said unto me, The Lord, before whom I walk, will send His angel with thee, and prosper thy way, that thou mayest take a wife for my son, of my kindred, and of my father's house.

Then when thou comest to my kindred, and if they do not give thee one, thou shalt be clear from thy oath.

And I came this day unto the well, and said, O Lord God of my master Abraham, if now thou do prosper the way which I go, behold, I stand by the well of water, and it shall come to pass that the virgin who cometh forth to draw water, and I say to her, Give me, I pray thee, a little water from thy pitcher to drink; and she say to me, Both drink thou, and I will draw water for thy camels also: let the same be the woman whom the Lord hath appointed for my master's son.

And before I had done speaking, Rebekah came forth, with her pitcher on her shoulder, and she went down unto the well and drew water, and I said unto her, Let me drink, I pray thee; and she made haste and let down her pitcher from her shoulder and said, Drink, and I will give thy camels drink also.

And I asked her, Whose daughter art thou? and she told me. And I put the earrings in her ear, and the bracelet upon her arm, and I bowed down my head and blessed the Lord God of my master Abraham, which had led me in the right way to take my master's brother's daughter unto his son.

And now, if ye will deal kindly and truly with my master, tell me: and if not tell me; that I may turn to the right hand or to the left.

Then Laban and Bethuel answered and said, The thing proceedeth from the Lord; we cannot speak unto thee, bad or good. Behold, Rebekah is before thee; take her, and go, and let her be thy master's son's wife, as the Lord hath spoken.

And it came to pass that when Abraham's servant heard these words, he worshipped the Lord, bowing himself to the earth.

And he brought forth jewels of silver, and jewels of gold, and gave them to Rebekah; he gave also to her mother and to her brother precious things.

And they did eat and drink, he and the men that were with him, and tarried all night; and they rose up in the morning, and he said:

Send me away unto my master; but her mother and brother said, Let the damsel abide with us a few days, at the least ten; after that she shall go.

And he said, Hinder me not, seeing the Lord hath prospered my way; send me away that I may go to my master. And they said, We will call the damsel and inquire at her own mouth.

And they called Rebekah, and said unto her, Wilt thou go with this man? And she said, I will go.

And they sent away Rebekah, and her nurse, and Abraham's servant, and his men.

And they blessed Rebekah, and said, Thou art our kinswoman, be thou the mother of thousands of millions, and let thy seed possess the gate of them that hate them.

And Rebekah arose, and her damsels, and they rode upon camels, and followed the man, and went on their way.

And Isaac came from the way of the well Lahairoi; for he dwelt in the south country.

And he went into the field to meditate at eventide; and he lifted up his eyes, and, behold, he saw the camels coming.

And Rebekah lifted up her eyes, and when she saw Isaac, she lighted off the camel, and took a veil and covered herself; for she had said unto the servant, What man is this that walketh in the field to meet us? And the servant had said, It is my master's son.

And he told Isaac all things that he had done.

And Isaac brought Rebekah into his mother's tent, and she became his wife, and he loved her, and was comforted after his mother's death.

CONVERSATION XIV.

Mamma.—When Abraham's servant had told his errand, and related all the circumstances of his journey, how did Laban and Bethuel answer his request that they would deal kindly with his master?

Ada.—They said, " The thing proceedeth from the Lord: we cannot speak unto thee bad or good. Behold, Rebekah is before thee, take her, and go, and let her be thy master's son's wife, as the Lord hath spoken."

Esther.—I do not not remember reading that God told Laban and Bethuel to let Rebekah go.

Mamma.—The words of our text do not mean that God spoke directly to Laban or Bethuel, but the manner in which Eleazar's prayer was answered showed so plainly that Rebekah had been chosen by God to be Isaac's wife, that they were convinced they ought to let her go.

Ada.—Does it not seem strange that Rebekah was willing to leave her home so immediately?

Mamma.—Under ordinary circumstances, it would certainly appear unnatural that she should have consented to go with a stranger, to marry a man whom she had never seen; but doubtless she had already heard of Abraham, and the promises God had made to him, and felt grateful to God that she had been chosen to be the mother of a nation whose noble destiny was foretold.

Esther.—Then you think she did right to leave her mother?

Mamma.—I think the events showed so clearly God's special providence towards her, that had she shown any hesitation, it would have appeared like unwillingness to obey His commands. What are we told that Rebekah did when she learned that it was Isaac she saw in the field?

Esther.—She covered herself with a veil.

Mamma.—You may notice here that it was the custom for a bride to be veiled in the time of Abraham, as it is in the present day. What do we read of Isaac?

Ada.—That he was walking in the field to meditate at eventide. I have thought sometimes, dear Mamma, that these words might mean that he was in prayer.

Mamma.—I cannot assert that you are correct my dear child, but I am very pleased that you have formed the same idea on the subject as myself. The evening hour, at the close of a hot summer day, is a most appropriate one for contemplating the beauties of nature; thus rendering silent adoration to our Maker, and giving Him the prayer of the heart, even when words do not pass our lips. This chapter of our Bible has always appeared to me as one of its most beautiful pictures.

Esther.—Pictures, dear Mamma? What do you mean? Our Bibles have not always pictures.

Mamma.—I did not mean painted pictures, my darling but images which *words* raise in our minds. When you read, do you not fancy that you see the people and the places that are described?

Esther.—O yes, Mamma, I fancy I see Isaac in the field, and the camels with Rebekah and Eleazar coming towards him.

Mamma.—And can you not fancy, also, that you see Isaac walking sadly and quietly in the stillness of the evening; that you can almost see how he is thinking of the dear mother whose death he has not yet ceased to mourn; that he is calming his thoughts with a prayer to his Maker, and meditating upon the beauties of nature?

Ada.—Indeed, Mamma, this is beautifully described in our Bible, and yet the words are very simple.

Mamma.—That is one of the great beauties of our Bible, both of the original in Hebrew and the English version of the text.

Ada.—And are we not shown forcibly Isaac's great love for his mother?

Mamma.—Yes, my dear; I do not think any words

could possibly be chosen, that could express more beautifully Isaac's feelings for both his mother and his wife. Can you repeat them?

Ada.—It is written, "And Isaac loved her, and was comforted after his mother's death."

READING XV.

Then Abraham took another wife whose name was Keturah, and she bare him many sons.

And Abraham gave all that he had unto his son Isaac; but unto his other sons Abraham gave presents, and sent them away from Isaac his son while he yet lived, into the east country.

And Abraham lived an hundred and three score and fifteen years, and died in a good old age, and was gathered to his people.

And his sons, Isaac and Ishmael, buried him in the cave in the field of Ephron, where Sarah also was buried.

And it came to pass, that after the death of Abraham, God greatly blessed Isaac, and he still dwelt by the well Lahairoi.

And Ishmael became the father of twelve princes, who had in possession castles, and towns, and nations, and they dwelt from Havilah unto Shur that is before Egypt.

And Ishmael died in the presence of all his brethren, and was gathered unto his people, being an hundred and thirty and seven years.

And Isaac was forty years old when he took Rebekah to wife.

And Isaac entreated the Lord for Rebekah, because she had no child; and the Lord heard him, and told Rebekah that she should at once become the mother of two sons, who should be the heads of two nations; and that the elder should serve the younger.

And when the first was born, he was red and hairy, and she called his name Esau.

And when the second was born, he took hold of his brother's heel, and they called his name Jacob. Then was Isaac three score years old.

And the boys grew, and Esau became a cunning hunter, and Jacob was a plain man, dwelling in tents.

And Isaac loved Esau, because he ate of his venison; but Rebekah loved Jacob.

And Jacob made pottage, and Esau said unto Jacob, Feed me, I pray thee, with that same red pottage, for I am faint; therefore was he named Edom.

And Jacob answered him, Sell me this day thy birthright.

And Esau said, Behold I am at the point of death, then what profit will this birthright do me should I die?

And Jacob said, Swear to me this day. And he sware unto him, and he sold his birthright unto Jacob.

Then Jacob gave Esau bread and pottage of lentiles, and he did eat and drink, and rose up and went his way.

Thus Esau despised his birthright.

CONVERSATION XV.

Mamma.—Had Abraham any other children besides Isaac and Ishmael?

Esther.—Yes, he had several, but you did not tell us their names, dear Mamma?

Mamma.—I did not read you all their names, my darling, because I thought you would scarcely remember them at present. When you are older you will be able to read them in the large Bible for yourself.

Esther.—Why did Abraham send all his sons away from him, except Isaac?

Mamma.—I think he was fearful lest, after his death, they might dispute with Isaac for equal shares of his property; and it was intended that Isaac should inherit the whole. Abraham, therefore, made each of his sons presents in his lifetime, instead of waiting until after his death. Can you remember the words of the texts in which Abraham's death is related?

Ada.—" And Abraham lived an hundred and three score years, and was gathered to his people."

Mamma.—Do either of you understand the meaning of the words " was gathered to his people."

Ada.—It means that he died.

Mamma.—Truly, it is the method of relating Abraham's death, and is an expression which is often used instead of saying of a person, " he died;" but, it seems to imply much more than the mere fact of death.

Ada.—I do not quite understand you, Mamma. I thought this was merely an *idiom* of the eastern language.

Mamma.—We may call it so if we please, but does not this idiom of the language, this form of speech show that there was an existing belief at the time our Bible was written, in the immortality of the soul?

Ada.—How does this passage show the belief, Mamma? It does not appear quite clear to me.

Mamma.—Have you not observed, my dear, that Abraham died far away from the graves of his own kindred. Sarah was the first who was buried in the cave of Machpelah where Abraham's bones also lay; therefore, the expression, " gathered to his own people " cannot mean that his bones were laid with theirs, which naturally leads us to conclude that the words allude to the *soul, which is not confined to space,* and which it is supposed may rejoin the souls of those who have gone before.

Ada.—Thank you, dear Mamma, I understand this quite clearly now, and I am so glad you have told me of it, for do you know I heard it said the other day, that Jews did not believe in the immortality of the soul, and that there was no passage in our Bible that pointed it out.

Mamma.—My dear child, this is perhaps one of the least clear of the *many* which we find throughout our Bible. The idea appears to have been so generally received amongst us in all ages, that it was not necessary for Moses to make it known as a new fact. We must return to our history, for I think this conversation is a little too serious for Esther, although she is listening so intently. We must give her some questions. I know she likes to show me she has paid attention to our reading. Now, darling, How many sons had Ishmael?

Esther.—Twelve, who became princes, and possessed castles, towns, and nations.

Mamma.—How old was Isaac when he took Rebekah to wife?

Esther.—He was forty years old.

Mamma.—What prayer did Isaac offer to God?

Esther.—That He would give children to Rebekah and himself.

Mamma.—Relate to me what you remember about the children God gave them.

Esther.—They were named Jacob and Esau. Esau was red and hairy, and when they grew, Esau became a hunter; and Jacob remained at home and dwelt in a tent. And Jacob made pottage, and when Esau came in very hungry, he would not give him any until he promised to sell Jacob his birthright. Was not this very unkind of Jacob, Mamma? Do you not think he ought to have given Esau the pottage directly? Jacob was not a good man. Do you think he was, Mamma?

Mamma.—I do think, my darling, that Jacob would have acted in a much kinder and more brotherly manner had he given Esau the pottage without thinking of making any bargain with him. I should be sorry to see any of my little children acting in a similar way towards each other. You must not, however, think that Jacob was a bad man on account of this fault, and the few others of which we read Moses, in recording the history of the patriarchs, makes no attempt to conceal their faults, and if we read attentively, we shall find they never passed unpunished. But there must have been much good in Jacob's disposition, since we find that God assured him of His blessing and protection.

Esther.—Why did Jacob wish so much for the birthright?

Mamma.—If I answer this question according to our received ideas on the subject, you will perhaps consider the motive which we suppose to have actuated Jacob's conduct, as some palliation for his fault; but remember, my darling, I am not trying to justify the fault itself. We must never do wrong, however clear it may appear to our mind, that the one wrong act may lead to a good end. God will always bring the good to pass if He so wills it, without our intervention. But I have gone far away from our subject. I could not continue, for I was fearful to mislead you; try to remember what I have said. And now I will answer your question. You wished to know why Jacob was so anxious to possess the birthright? It was thought, that in the patriarchal times, that is, when each family was governed by its own head (the father having full control over all his children and servants) that the eldest son assumed the duties of priest, that he officiated at the sacrifices, and performed all the religious duties.

Esther.—You think then, Mamma, that Jacob wished to become the priest?

Mamma.—Yes, dear, I think it was this desire chiefly that made him so anxious to obtain the birthright, and I fancy that Esau had previously disregarded his duties, and thought very little of giving them up; for we are told, "Thus Esau despised his birthright," which words seem to show that he had very little regard for it, or would not have parted with it so easily.

Ada.—Do you not think, Mamma, that Esau was of a noble and generous disposition?

Mamma.—I think Esau's character was one which we are very apt to admire, but one which always does much harm to the person who possesses it, as well as to others. I fear he only thought at the moment of pleasing his inclinations, and in his case, as in the case of most impulsive people, the impulses are often good; but the want of self-control also causes them to do many things that are wrong. My darling, we have had a very long conversation to-day, and I fear you will not remember all we have been talking about.

Ada and Esther.—I am sure we will try, Mamma; we like these morning talks so much; we are always sorry when they are over.

READING XVI.

———o———

AND there was a famine in the land, besides the first famine that was in the days of Abraham.

And Isaac went unto Gerar; and the Lord appeared unto him, and said, Go not down into Egypt; dwell in the land which I shall tell thee of.

Sojourn in this land, and I will be with thee, and will bless thee; for unto thee and thy seed will I give all these countries, and I will perform the oath which I sware unto Abraham thy father; and I will make thy seed to multiply as the stars of heaven; and in thy seed shall all the nations of the earth be blessed.

Because that Abraham obeyed my voice and kept my charge, my commandments and my laws.

And Isaac dwelt in Gerar. And the men of the place asked him of his wife, and he said, she is my sister; for he feared to say she is my wife, lest, said he, the men of the place should kill me for Rebekah, because she is fair to look upon.

And it came to pass when he had been there a long time that the king of the Philistines saw Isaac sporting with Rebekah, as he looked out of his window.

And he called Isaac, and said, Behold of a surety she is thy wife, and how saidst thou she is my sister? And Isaac said, Because I thought I might die for her.

And the king said, What is this that thou hast done unto us? Thou mightest have brought guilt upon us. And he charged all his people, saying, He that toucheth this man or his wife shall surely be put to death.

Then Isaac sowed in the land and received in the same year an hundredfold; and the Lord blessed him.

And he waxed great, and went forward, until he became very great; for he had in possession flocks and herds, and a great store of servants; and the Philistines envied him.

And all the wells which his father's servants had digged, they had stopped and filled them with earth.

And the king said unto Isaac, Go from us, for thou art mightier than we.

And Isaac departed thence, and pitched his tent in the valley of Gerar, and dwelt there.

And Isaac opened again the wells which had been digged in the days of Abraham his father, and which the Philistines had filled up, and he called their names the same as his father had called them.

They likewise digged in the valley and found there a well of springing water, and the herdsmen of Gerar strove with Isaac's herdsmen, saying, The water is ours; and he called the name of the well Esek, because they strove with him.

And he digged another well, and they strove for that also; and he called the name of it Sitnah.

And they digged yet another well, and for that they strove not. And he called the name of it Rehoboth; and he said, For now the Lord hath made room for us, and we shall be fruitful in the land.

And Isaac went up from the valley of Gerar to Beersheba, and the Lord appeared to him the same night, and said, I am the God of thy father Abraham; fear not, for I am with thee, and will bless thee, and multiply thy seed, for my servant Abraham's sake.

And he builded an altar there, and called upon the name of the Lord, and pitched his tent there; and his servants digged there a well.

Then came the king of the Philistines and one of his friends, and the chief captain of his army from Gerar.

And Isaac said unto them, Wherefore come ye to me, seeing ye hate me, and have sent me away from you?

And they said, We saw certainly that the Lord was with thee; and we said let there be now an oath betwixt us and thee, and we will make a covenant with thee that thou wilt do us no hurt, as we have not touched thee, nor done anything but good unto thee, and have sent thee away in peace: thou art now one blessed of the Lord.

And Isaac made a feast, and they did eat and drink. And they arose up betimes in the morning, and sware one to another; and they departed from him in peace.

And on the same day Isaac's servants came and told him concerning the well which they had digged, saying, We have found water! And he called it Shebah; therefore the name of the city is Beershebah unto this day.

And when Esau was forty years old, he took for his wife Judith, the daughter of Beeri, the Hittite, and Bashemath, the daughter of Elon the Hittite; which grieved Isaac and Rebekah.

CONVERSATION XVI.

Mamma.—Why did Isaac remove to Gerar?

Esther.—Because there was a famine in the land.

Mamma.—Why did he not proceed to Egypt as he had intended?

Esther.—Because God appeared to him, and told him to remain in Gerar.

Mamma.—It was at this time that God appeared to Isaac, and renewed the promise He had made to Abraham; that the whole world should be blessed through his descendants. God also told Isaac His reason for conferring this great blessing. Can you repeat the words of the text?

Ada.—"Because that Abraham obeyed my voice, and kept my commandments and my laws."

Mamma.—When Isaac was asked by the men of the plain about his wife, what did he say?

Esther.—He said she is my sister. Is it not strange, Mamma dear, that he should have committed the same fault as Abraham? Do you not think he ought to have learned to place more faith in God?

Mamma.—It is a strange coincidence; but you must not think Isaac's fault was greater than Abraham's. I see you are thinking that Isaac ought to have profited by Abraham's experience; but although *we* know all that happened to Abraham, it is not quite certain that Isaac did so, Moses may have recorded events that Abraham had not told to Isaac.

Esther.—I did not think of that, Mamma.

Mamma.—Did Isaac remain at Gerar after he became rich and powerful?

Esther.—No; the men of the place asked him to remove, because he had become mightier than they.

Mamma.—What are we next told of Isaac?

Esther.—That he opened the wells which his father had digged, and which the Philistines had stopped.

Mamma.—Do you remember the names by which Isaac called the wells his servants digged, and his reasons for so calling them?

Ada.—He called the first עֵשֶׂק (I-sek), which means strife, and the second שִׂטְנָה Sit-nah, which means contention, because the herdsmen of Gerar strove with his servants for both of them. The third Isaac called רְחֹבוֹת (Re-chow-bous), which means room, for the herdsmen strove not for this one, therefore Isaac said, "The Lord hath made room for us."

Mamma.—Have you remarked that the relation of these circumstances, prove Isaac to have been of a remarkably peaceful disposition, and also shew how entirely he ascribed all his success in life to God.

Ada.—I have noticed that he must have been very unwilling to quarrel; but what do you mean, Mamma, by saying that his entire reliance on God is proved by these circumstances?

Mamma.—I mean, dear, that the name he gave to the last well proves his acknowledgment that he owed all things to God, for he did not say now we have succeeded in obtaining peace, but, "Now God hath made room for us." Thus the name stood as a record of Isaac's thankfulness to his Maker. We next read of the visit of the king of the Philistines to Isaac, and the treaty made between them. Have you any recollection of having already read of similar events?

Esther.—O yes, Mamma, I remember that almost the same circumstances occurred to Abraham; and the name Abraham called the well was the same. The only difference, I remember, between the two histories is, that Isaac made a feast, and Abraham gave seven lambs as a present to Abimelech.

Mamma.—What do we learn next of Esau?

Esther.—That he married Judith and Bashemath, both daughters of the children of Heth.

Mamma.—And, that this was a grief of mind to Isaac and to Rebekah. No doubt these women were the daughters of idolaters. Thus, we learn, that Isaac, like his father Abraham, considered it wrong for his children to intermarry with strangers, lest they might be led away from the worship of the true God, and the observance of His commands, and, to the present day, the same practice is to be avoided.

READING XVII.

———o———

And it came to pass, that when Isaac was old, and his eyes were dim, so that he could not see, he called Esau, his eldest son, and said unto him, My son! And he said unto him, Behold here am I.

And Isaac said, Behold now I am old, I know not the day of my death; now then take thy quiver and thy bow, and go out to the field, and take me some venison, and dress me savoury meat such as I love, and bring it to me that I may eat; that my soul may bless thee before I die.

And Rebekah heard when Isaac spake to Esau his son.

And Esau went to the field to hunt for venison, and to bring it.

And Rebekah spake unto Jacob her son, saying, Behold I heard thy father speak unto Esau, thy brother, saying, Bring me venison, and make me savoury meat, that I may eat, and bless thee, before I die.

Now therefore my son, obey my voice according to that which I command thee: Go now to the flock, and fetch me two kids of the goats, and I will make them savoury meat for thy father, such as he loveth. And thou shalt bring it to thy father that he may eat, and that his soul may bless thee before his death.

And Jacob said unto Rebekah his mother, Behold, Esau my brother is a hairy man, and I am a smooth man: my father may feel me, and I shall seem to him as a deceiver; and I shall bring a curse upon me instead of a blessing.

And his mother said unto him, Upon me be thy curse, my son; only obey my voice and go and fetch me them.

And he went and took them, and brought them to his mother; and she made savoury meat, such as his father loved.

And Rebekah took goodly raiment of her eldest son Esau, and put them upon Jacob her youngest son. And she put skins of the kids upon his hands, and upon the smooth of his neck. And she gave the savoury meat, and the bread that she had prepared, into the hand of her son Jacob.

And he came unto his father, and said, My father! And Isaac said, Who art thou, my son? And Jacob said unto his father, I am Esau thy firstborn; I have done according as thou didst command me: arise, I pray thee, sit and eat of my venison, that thy soul may bless me.

And Isaac said, How is it that thou hast found it so quickly, my son? And he said, Because the Lord thy God brought it to me.

And Isaac said, Come near that I may feel thee, whether thou be my son Esau or not.

And Jacob went near unto his father, and he felt him, and said, The voice is Jacob's voice, but the hands are the hands of Esau. And he discerned him not, because his hands were hairy, as his brother Esau's hands. So he blessed him.

And he said, Art thou my very son Esau? and he said, I am. And Isaac said, Bring it near to me, and I will eat of my son's venison, that my soul may bless thee.

And he brought it near to him, and he did eat; and he brought him wine and he drank and said unto Jacob, Come near now and kiss me, my son.

And he came near to him, and he kissed him, and he smelled his raiment, and blessed him, and said, The smell of my son is as the smell of a field which the Lord hath blessed.

Therefore God give thee of the dew of heaven, and the fatness of the earth, and plenty of corn and wine: let people serve thee, and nations bow down to thee:

Be lord over thy brethren, and let thy mother's sons bow down to thee:

Cursed be every one that curseth thee, and blessed be he that blesseth thee.

CONVERSATION XVII.

Mamma.—When Isaac was old, and his eyes were dim, what did he desire of Esau?

Esther.—He called Esau and desired him to go and hunt for venison to make savoury meat, that he might eat of it and bless him before he died.

Mamma.—Do you know what venison is, Esther?

Esther.—Yes, dear Mamma, it is the flesh of deer. Why do we never eat of it, if it is a clean animal?

Mamma.—Because, in this country, the deer are not allowed to be caught and brought to market alive, and we only eat of such animals as we know to have been killed properly. Can you tell me what is next related of Jacob?

Esther.—Yes, Rebekah called Jacob and told him to fetch her some kids, that she might imitate the venison, and that he should go in to Isaac to receive the blessing intended for Esau. It was very wrong of Jacob to deceive his father, but I do not think it was quite his fault; Rebekah ought not to have told him to do so.

Mamma.—You are quite correct, my darling; it does not appear that Jacob was quite willing to become a party to this fraud, for he said to his mother, that he would appear as a deceiver, and bring a curse instead of a blessing upon himself; and she entreated Jacob to obey her voice, saying that she would take the curse upon herself; and indeed she suffered severely from this act, for in consequence of it, Jacob was obliged to leave home.

Ada.—Do you think, Mamma, that Rebekah did so very wrong to try to secure the blessing for Jacob? Might she not have thought that she was right to do anything that would cause the prophecy to be fulfilled which was made known to her, before the birth of Jacob and Esau?

Mamma.—I cannot say, my dear child, but that Rebekah may have been actuated by this motive, and I am glad to see you inclined to judge charitably of the failings of others; but you must be careful in guiding your own conduct by their example, not to make the failings of great characters excuses for ourselves. I again impress upon you that we must "never do evil that good may come," however great or good the end we hope to gain by the one wrong act. God doubtless would have fulfilled His promise had the mother and son not resorted to this stratagem, and Rebekah would have been spared the pain of parting from her favorite son. Jacob paid the penalty of his share in the deception, by a long and painful exile from his home and country.

Ada.—It does not appear that Isaac was very easily deceived; he seems to have had great doubt that it was Jacob instead of Esau speaking to him.

Mamma.—Yes, my dear, and you may perceive that although Jacob imitated his brother's appearance, he had not imitated his voice and manner. The expression by which he answers his father's question, as to how he found the venison so quickly, we should not expect to find uttered by Esau, who appears to have been of a reckless and thoughtless disposition.

Esther.—You mean, Mamma, when Jacob said God had brought it to him.

Mamma.—Yes, my dear; do you remember the words in which Isaac expresses his doubts?

Esther.—Yes, Mamma; he said, "The voice is the voice of Jacob, but the hands are the hands of Esau."

Mamma.—In what manner could Isaac distinguish the hands of Esau from the hands of Jacob?

Esther.—Esau's hands were hairy, whilst those of Jacob were smooth, therefore Rebekah put the skins of the kids upon Jacob's hands.

Mamma.—Can you remember the words of Isaac's blessing to Jacob?

Ada.—Isaac said, "The smell of my son is as the smell

of a field which the Lord hath blessed. Therefore God give thee of the dew of heaven and the fatness of the earth, and plenty of corn and wine; let people serve thee and nations bow down to thee: be lord over thy brethren, and let thy mother's sons bow down to thee: cursed be every one that curseth thee, and blessed be he that blesseth thee."

READING XVIII.

———o———

AND it came to pass as soon as Isaac had made an end of blessing Jacob, and he had scarce gone out from the presence of his father, that Esau, his brother, came in from hunting. And he also dressed savoury meat, and brought it to his father, and said, Let my father arise, and eat of his son's venison that thy soul may bless me.

And Isaac his father said unto him, Who art thou? and he said, I am thy son, thy firstborn, Esau.

And Isaac trembled, and said, Who? Where is he that hath brought me venison, and I have eaten of it before thou camest, and have blessed him? Yea, and he shall be blessed.

And when Esau heard the words of his father, he cried with an exceeding bitter cry, and said unto his father, Bless me, even me also, O my father!

And he said, Thy brother came with subtlety and hath taken away thy blessing.

And Esau said, Is he not rightly called Jacob? for he hath supplanted me these two times: he took away my birthright, and behold, now, he hath taken away my blessing. And he said, Hast thou not reserved a blessing for me?

And Isaac answered, and said unto Esau, Behold, I have made him thy lord, and all his brethren have I given to him for servants, and with corn and wine have I sustained him; and what shall I do now unto thee, my son?

And Esau said unto his father, Hast thou but one blessing, my father? Bless me, even me also, O my father! And Esau lifted up his voice and wept.

And Isaac his father answered him and said, Behold thy dwelling shall be the fatness of the earth, and of the dew of heaven from above; and by thy sword shalt thou live, and shalt serve thy brother. And it shall come to pass that thou shalt break his yoke from off thy neck.

And Esau hated Jacob because of the blessing wherewith his father blessed him, and he said The days of mourning for my father are at hand; then will I slay my brother Jacob.

And these words of Esau were told to Rebekah, and she said unto Jacob, Thy brother Esau doth comfort himself, purposing to kill thee.

Now therefore, my son, obey my voice: Arise, and flee to my brother Laban, to Haran, and tarry with him till thy brother's fury be turned away, and he forget that which thou hast done to him: then I will send and fetch thee; why should I be deprived of thy father and thee in one day?

And Rebekah said unto Isaac, I am weary of my life, because of the daughters of Heth. If Jacob take a wife of these, the daughters of the land, what good shall my life do me?

Then Isaac called Jacob and blessed him, and charged him, saying, Thou shalt not take a wife of the daughters of Canaan.

Arise, go to Padan Aram, to the house of thy mother's brother, and there take a wife of the daughters of Laban.

And God Almighty bless thee, and make thee fruitful and multiply thee, and give thee the blessing of Abraham, that thou mayest inherit the land wherein thou art a stranger, which God gave unto Abraham.

And Isaac sent away Jacob, and he went unto Padan Aram to Laban his uncle.

And when Esau saw that the daughters of Canaan pleased not his father and his mother, he went and took Mahalath, the daughter of Ishmael, to be his wife.

CONVERSATION XVIII.

Mamma.—What happened immediately after Jacob had left his father's presence?

Esther.—Esau came in with the savoury meat which he had prepared.

Mamma.—Can you tell me what is related of Isaac, when he discovered the deception that had been practised on him?

Ada.—It is written, "and Isaac trembled exceedingly, and said, Who? Where is he that hath brought me venison, and I have eaten of it before thou camest, and have blessed him? Yea, and he shall be blessed."

Esther.—But, Mamma, could not Isaac have taken the blessing away from Jacob and have given it to Esau?

Mamma.—It appears not, my dear; from Isaac's manner and words as here described, he must have been under the influence of the prophetic spirit, for the words, "Yea, and he shall be blessed," do not appear to have been uttered of his own will.

Esther.—Do you mean that it was not in the power of Isaac to say what he wished?

Mamma.—Yes, my dear; I think he was inspired with the words, which it was God's will he should pronounce; for the blessing he gave his children was not immediate, but pointed to the future, of which he could know nothing.

Esther.—I do not quite understand you, dear Mamma.

Mamma.—Do you not know that, immediately after receiving his father's blessing, Jacob became a wanderer and an exile? that he remained in servitude many years? Thus he suffered full punishment, and did not reap any advantage from his deceitful conduct, while Esau was at this time superior in power to himself; the blessing, therefore, plainly alludes to what should happen in futurity to the descendants of both. Isaac told Esau that "he should break his brother's yoke from off his neck," which event occurred at a later period of our history, when the Edomites, or descendants of Esau, actually freed themselves from the dominion of the Israelites.

Esther.—I did not know this, Mamma, and it appeared to me that it was not right that Jacob should profit through his bad conduct.

Mamma.—My dear child, there are many things related to us in the Bible, and also many things which occur in our every-day life, that do not at first sight appear to us in accordance with the justice of God. His decrees we must not question. It is sin to think of our Creator as of a being who is not *all perfection*. If we are sometimes puzzled with questions which we cannot reconcile to our own minds, we must ascribe our difficulties either to our own finite judgment, or to a want of knowledge of all the circumstances.

Esther.—May I not enquire of you, dear Mamma, if anything in the Bible does not appear to me quite right?

Mamma.—You certainly may, my darling; I wish you to bring to me every question that arises in your mind, but you must not feel disappointed if I cannot always give you a reason for everything. Do not question in a spirit of doubt, but with the desire to reconcile to your mind the ways of God, which you must feel certain are just and right, although beyond our immediate comprehension.

Ada.—Esau appears to have felt great affection for his father, and to have earnestly desired his blessing. The words in which he addresses his father are really very touching.

Mamma.—They are indeed, my child. Esau doubtless possessed some fine and generous qualities; his conduct towards his brother which we shall read of by and bye, was noble and forgiving. He also seems to have had some desire to atone for the grief he caused his father and mother by marrying strange wives. Do you remember the name of the third wife he took?

Esther.—Yes, Mahalath, the daughter of Ishmael.

Mamma.—What excuse did Rebekah make to Isaac, in

order that he might send Jacob away to avoid his brother's fury?

Esther.—She said, Lest he should marry, as Esau had done, women of the land in which they dwelt, and that this would be a great grief to her.

Mamma.—Where did Isaac then tell Jacob to go?

Esther.—To Padan Aram, where dwelt Laban his mother's brother?

READING XIX.

And as Jacob went out from Beersheba towards Haran, he lighted upon a certain place, and tarried there all night, because the sun was set; and he took one of the stones of that place, and put it for his pillow, and laid down to sleep.

And he dreamed, and behold a ladder set upon the earth, and the top of it reached to heaven; and behold the angels of God were ascending and descending upon it.

And, behold, the Lord stood above it, and said, I am the Lord God of Abraham thy father, and the God of Isaac: the land whereon thou liest, to thee will I give it, and to thy seed.

And thy seed shall be as the dust of the earth, and thou shalt spread abroad to the west, and to the east, and to the north, and to the south: and in thee and thy seed shall all the nations of the earth be blessed.

And, behold, I am with thee, and will keep thee in all places whither thou goest, and I will bring thee again into this land; for I will not leave thee, until I have done that which I have spoken to thee of.

And Jacob awaked out of his sleep, and said, Surely the Lord is in this place, and I knew it not. How awful is this place! it is none other but the house of God, and this is the gate of heaven. And he was afraid.

And he rose early in the morning, and took the stone which he had for his pillow, and set it up for a pillar, and poured oil upon the top of it. And he called the name of that place Bethel.

And Jacob vowed unto the Lord, saying, If God will be with me, and will keep me in this way that I go, and will give me bread to eat, and raiment to put on, so that I come again to my father's house in peace, then shall the Lord be my God: and of all that thou shalt give me, I will surely give the tenth unto thee; and this stone, which I have set for a pillar, shall be God's house.

Then he went on his journey, and came unto the east country, and looked and beheld a well in a field. And there were flocks of sheep lying by it, and a stone upon the well's mouth. And thither were all the flocks gathered for water.

And the men of the place came and rolled the stone from the mouth of the well, and watered the sheep, and put the stone again upon the well.

And Jacob said unto them, My brethren, whence be ye? And they said, Of Haran are we. And he said unto them, Know ye Laban the son of Nahor? And they said, We know him. And he said, Is he well? And they said, He is well; and, behold, Rachel his daughter cometh with the sheep.

And he said, Lo, it is yet high day, neither is it time that the cattle should be gathered together; water ye the sheep, and go and feed them.

And while he yet spake to them, Rachel came with her father's sheep, for she kept them. And when Jacob saw Rachel he went near, and rolled the stone from the well's mouth, and watered the flock of Laban, his mother's brother.

And Jacob kissed Rachel, and lifted up his voice, and wept. And he told Rachel that he was Rebekah's son; and she ran and told her father.

And when Laban heard the tidings of his sister's son he ran to meet Jacob and embraced him, and kissed him, and brought him to his house.

And Laban said, Surely thou art my bone, and my

flesh; and he abode with him a month. And at the end of that time, Laban said unto Jacob,

Because thou art my nephew, shouldst thou therefore serve me for nought? Tell me, what shall thy wages be? And Jacob said, I will serve thee seven years for Rachel, thy younger daughter.

Now Laban had two daughters; the name of the elder was Leah, and she was tender eyed; but Rachel, the younger, was beautiful and well favoured. And Jacob loved Rachel.

And Laban said, It is better that I give her unto thee than to another: abide then with me.

CONVERSATION XIX.

Mamma.—When Jacob laid down and slept in the road between Beersheba and Haran, what did he dream?

Esther.—He dreamt that he saw a ladder, whose top reached to heaven, and that the angels of God were ascending and descending upon it.

Mamma.—Was there not something more that was remarkable in this dream?

Ada.—Yes, God renewed the promise to Jacob that He had made to Abraham and to Isaac.

Mamma.—This dream of Jacob's is considered as prophetic of God's especial care of the children of Jacob throughout all generations. What nation is descended from Jacob?

Ada.—Our own—the Jews or Israelites; but, dear Mamma, we are no longer a nation.

Mamma.—Truly, my dear, we have now no kings or rulers of our own, and are scattered all over the earth; but we still remain, in every country where we sojourn, as distinct a people as we were in our own land. We are "a nation in the midst of nations unto this day," and are even now fulfilling the mission of Abraham, blessing all the nations of the earth. Can you tell me in what manner?

Ada.—I think you told us before, dear Mamma, that we blessed other nations by teaching them, through our example, the worship of the true God.

Mamma.—Yes, my dear, and by showing the world at large that the observance of the commands of God must make men better, truer, and happier in every sense of the words; therefore, we Jews and Jewesses should be most careful in all our actions, for if we fail in our duties we bring discredit upon our nation, and upon our holy law as well as upon ourselves and our families. Now, tell me Esther, the name Jacob gave to the place where he had slept?

Esther.—He called it בֵּית־אֵל (Bes-ïl), which means the House of God.

Mamma.—Do you remember the vow Jacob made at this time?

Ada.—He vowed that if God would provide for him, and bring him back in peace to his father's house, he would devote to God's service the tenth part of all that God should give him.

Mamma.—Do you know that to the present day our people consider it right to devote the tenth part of their possessions to the service of God? — that is to say, to give away that amount in charity; for it is only by helping those of our fellow-creatures who may be poorer than ourselves, that we can show our gratitude to God for the blessings He bestows upon us.

Esther.—Why did Jacob pour oil upon the stone?

Mamma.—To consecrate the place; it was an Eastern custom to pour oil upon anything which was to be consecrated to God's service; thus the kings and priests were anointed with oil. Jacob vowed that if God would bring him back in safety, he would worship Him in this place; he set up the stone that he might be enabled to distinguish it, for having been favoured there by a vision from God, he fancied it peculiarly holy. It is supposed that the tabernacle was erected upon this spot. Is there not yet something which we may remark of Jacob's conduct?

Ada.—You mean, dear Mamma, that he merely asked of God safety and the necessaries of life.

Mamma.—When Jacob perceived Rachel, what did he do?

Esther.—He rolled the stone from the well's mouth and then ran to meet her, kissed her, and told her that he was Rebekah's son.

Mamma.—What relations were Jacob and Rachel?

I

Esther.—They were cousins.

Mamma.—For what wages did Jacob say that he would serve Laban, his uncle, for seven years?

Esther.—He said he would remain with him, and serve him, if Laban would give him his younger daughter, Rachel, to wife.

READING XX.

And Jacob served seven years for Rachel, and they seemed unto him only as a few days, for the great love he had unto her.

And he said unto Laban, Give me my wife, for my days are fulfilled that I may take her.

And Laban gathered together all the young men of the place and made a feast.

And in the evening Laban took Leah, his elder daughter, and brought her to Jacob, and gave unto her Zilpah for a handmaid.

And in the morning Jacob said unto Laban, What is this that thou hast done unto me? Did I not serve thee for Rachel? Wherefore then hast thou deceived me?

And Laban answered, It must not be so done in our country, to give the younger before the elder. Fulfil the week of this, and serve me other seven years, and thou shalt have the younger also, even before thou servest.

And after a week he gave him Rachel, his daughter, also to wife, and Bilhah to be her handmaid.

And Jacob served Laban other seven years for Rachel, and he loved her more than Leah.

And God gave Leah a son, and she called his name Reuben, for she said God hath looked upon my affliction. Now, therefore, my husband will love me. And again she bare another son, and said, Because God knew that I was hated, He hath, given me this son also. And she called his name Simeon.

And she had another son, and said, Now this time will my husband love me because I have borne him three sons, and she called him Levi.

And she again bare a son, and said, Now will I praise the Lord; therefore she called his name Judah.

And when Rachel saw that she had no children, she was grieved, and gave unto Jacob her handmaid to wife; and she bare him a son, and Rachel called his name Dan. And Bilhah bare Jacob a second son, and Rachel called his name Naphthali.

And when Leah saw that she had no more children, she gave to Jacob Zilpah, her handmaid, to wife, and she bare a son, and Leah called his name Gad. And Zilpah bare Jacob a second son, and Leah called his name Asher.

Then Leah bare a fifth son, and she called his name Issachar. And yet another, and she called him Zebulon.

And afterwards she bare a daughter, and called her name Dinah.

Then God remembered Rachel, and gave her a son of her own. And she said, God hath taken away my reproach, and she called his name Joseph, and said, The Lord will add to me another son.

And it came to pass after the birth of Joseph, that Jacob said unto Laban, Send me away that I may go to my own place and to my country. Give me my wives, and my children, for whom I have served thee, and let me go, for thou knowest my service which I have done thee.

And Laban said unto him, I pray thee if I have found favour in thine eyes, tarry, for I have learned that God hath blessed me for thy sake. Appoint me thy wages, and I will give it.

And Jacob answered, Thou knowest how I have served thee, and how thy cattle was with me, for it was little that thou hadst when I came, and it is now increased into a multitude, and how God hath blessed thee since my coming, and now when shall I provide for my own house also?

And Laban said, What shall I give thee?

And Jacob said, Thou shalt not give me anything. If thou wilt do this thing for me, I will again feed and keep thy flock.

I will pass through all thy flock to-day and remove from thence all the speckled and spotted cattle, and all the brown among the sheep, and the speckled and spotted among the goats; and of such shall be my hire: and this shall be my right in time to come. But every one that is not speckled and spotted among the cattle, and brown among the sheep, shall be thine.

And Laban said, Behold, let it be according to thy word. And that day Jacob removed all the cattle and the goats that were speckled, and all the brown among the sheep, and gave them into the hands of his sons, and Laban sent them three days' journey off his own flocks. And Jacob fed the rest of Laban's flock.

And after this the greater number of the cattle brought forth their young ones ringstraked, speckled and spotted.

And Jacob heard Laban's sons, saying, Jacob hath taken all that was our father's, and of that which was our father's hath he gotten all this glory. And Jacob beheld the countenance of Laban, that it was not towards him as before.

And the Lord said unto Jacob, Return unto the land of thy fathers, and to thy kindred, and I will be with thee.

And Jacob sent and called Rachel and Leah into

the field where he was with the flocks, and said unto them, I see your father that his countenance is not towards me as before, but the God of my fathers has been with me.

And ye know that with all my power I have served your father, and he hath deceived me, and changed my wages ten times ; but God suffered him not to hurt me.

If he said thus, The speckled shall be thy wages, then all the cattle bare speckled ; and if he said, The ringstraked shall be thy hire, then bare all the cattle ringstraked.

Thus God hath taken the cattle of your father, and hath given them to me.

And the angel of God spake unto me in a dream, saying Jacob, and I said, Here am I. And he said, I have seen all that Laban doeth unto thee.

I am the God of Bethel, where thou anointedst the pillar, and where thou vowedst unto me. Now, arise, get thee out of this land, and return unto the land of thy kindred.

And Rachel and Leah said unto him, Is there yet any portion or inheritance for us in our father's house? Hath he not sold us and altogether devoured our money. For all the riches which God hath taken from our father is ours and our children's.

Now, then, whatsoever God hath said unto thee, do.

CONVERSATION XX.

———o———

Mamma.—Can you tell me how many years Jacob served Laban for Rachel, and what is remarked concerning this service?

Esther.—Seven years; and it is written that "they appeared to him as a few days only, on account of the great love he had for her."

Mamma.—What excuse did Laban make to Jacob for having deceived him, in giving him Leah instead of Rachel?

Ada.—He said that it was against the custom of the country, that the younger daughter should marry before the elder one.

Mamma.—What agreement did Laban and Jacob make after this?

Esther.—That Jacob should serve another seven years, and that Laban would give him Rachel also.

Mamma.—Whom did Laban give his daughters for handmaids?

Esther.—Bilhah and Zilpah.

Mamma.—Give me the names of Leah's children.

Esther.—Reuben, Simeon, Levi, Judah, Issachar, and Zebulon.

Mamma.—The children of Bilhah?

Esther.—Dan and Naphtali.

Mamma.—Of Zilpah?

Esther.—Gad and Asher.

Mamma.—Of Rachel?

Esther.—Joseph.

Mamma.—And Benjamin, but he was not born until after Jacob had left Laban. These sons of Jacob became the heads of the twelve tribes of Israel. Joseph's inheritance however, was divided into two, both his sons Ephraim and Manasseh, becoming heads of tribes; but of this we shall read later.

Esther.—Mamma, how was it that Jacob did not know that it was Leah instead of Rachel who was brought to him?

Mamma.—Because in the country in which these events occurred, it was the custom for the bride to be closely veiled during the marriage ceremony, and to be conducted to her husband's tent without having raised her veil. You must remember that Rebekah veiled herself when she saw Isaac approaching her. If we carefully study our Bible history, we learn, besides the important duties it teaches us, the customs of countries very different from the one in which we live.

Esther.—Was it not very wrong of Leah to help to deceive Jacob?

Mamma.—My dear child, we are not told that she willingly entered into the deception; we cannot judge of people's actions, unless we know the whole of the circumstances which influenced them.

Esther.—Then you do not think Leah was wicked?

Mamma.—I believe I have before desired you not to consider a person as wicked on account of one wrong action, and as we read more of Leah, and consider the signification of the names she gave her children, we find that she showed a truly religious spirit, for each of the names is expressive either of her gratitude to God, or reliance on His care for her. Did Laban wish Jacob to leave him after the marriage of his daughters?

Esther.—No; he saw that God blessed all that he had for Jacob's sake, and begged him to remain with him.

Mamma.—Upon what condition did Jacob consent?

Esther.—Upon condition that Laban would give him the spotted, speckled, and ringstraked from among the cattle.

Mamma.—What then happened?

Esther.—The greater portion and the best of the cattle bare spotted, speckled, and ringstraked.

Mamma.—When Laban's sons and Laban seemed to think that Jacob had acquired too much of their property, what did Jacob think of doing?

Esther.—Of returning to the land of Canaan.

Mamma.—How did he learn that it would be right for him to do so?

Ada.—An angel ot God appeared to him in a dream, and told him to return to the land of Canaan, and assured him of God's protection.

Mamma.—How did Leah and Rachel express themselves with regard to leaving their father's house?

Ada.—They were quite willing to remove, and said, "We have no longer any portion or inheritance in our father's house, for he has sold us, and altogether devoured our money."

READING XXI.

———o———

THEN Jacob rose up, and set his sons and his wives upon camels. And he carried away all his cattle, and all the goods which he had gotten in Haran, to go to Isaac his father in Canaan.

And Laban went to shear his sheep; and Rachel stole the images that were her father's. And Jacob stole away unawares, and fled with all that he had, and passed over the river, and set his face towards Mount Gilead.

And it was told Laban on the third day that Jacob was fled. And he took his brethren, and pursued after him, and overtook him after seven days' journey, on Mount Gilead.

And God spake to Laban, the Syrian, in a dream by night, and said unto him, Take heed that thou speak not to Jacob either good or bad.

When Laban overtook Jacob, he had pitched his tent in the mount, and Laban and his brethren pitched theirs also.

And Laban said unto Jacob, What hast thou done that thou hast stolen away unawares to me, and carried away my daughters as captives taken with the sword?

Wherefore didst thou flee away secretly; I might have sent thee away with mirth, and with songs, and with tabret, and with harp?

And thou hast not suffered me to kiss my sons and my daughters.

Thou hast done foolishly. It is in the power of my hand to do you hurt; but the God of your father spake to me yesternight, saying, Take thou heed that thou speak not to Jacob neither good nor bad.

And now, though thou wouldest need be gone, because thou greatly longest after thy father's house, yet wherefore hast thou stolen my gods?

And Jacob answered him, saying, I said perhaps thou wouldest take by force thy daughters from me. With whomsoever thou findest thy gods, let him not live (for he knew not that Rachel had stolen them): before our brethren claim thou what is thine with me, and take it to thee.

And Laban went into Jacob's tent, and into Leah's tent, and into the two handmaids' tents, but he found them not.

Then he went into Rachel's tent. Now Rachel had taken the images, and put them in the camel's furniture, and sat upon them. And Laban searched all the tent, but found them not.

Then Jacob was wroth with Laban, and said, What is my trespass? what is my sin? that thou hast so hotly pursued after me?

Thou hast searched all my household stuff, what hast thou found of thy household stuff? set it here before our brethren that they may judge betwixt us.

These twenty years have I been with thee; thy ewes and thy she goats have not cast their young, and the rams of thy flock have I not eaten. That which was torn of beasts I brought not unto thee; I bare the loss of it; of my hand didst thou require it, whether stolen by day or by night.

Thus I was; in the day the drought consumed me, and by night the frost; and my sleep departed from mine eyes.

I have served thee fourteen years for thy two daughters, and six years for thy cattle: and thou hast changed my wages ten times.

Except the God of my father, the God of Abraham, the Fear of Isaac, had been with me, surely thou hadst sent me away now empty. God hath seen my affliction, and the labour of my hands, and rebuked thee yesternight.

And Laban answered Jacob, saying, These daughters and children, and cattle, and all that thou seest are mine.

Now therefore come thou, let us make a covenant, I and thou; and let it be a witness between me and thee.

And Jacob took a stone, and set it up for a pillar. And Jacob said unto his brethren, Gather stones. And they took stones and made a heap, and did eat there upon the heap.

And Jacob called it Galeed; and Laban said, This heap is a witness between me and thee this day. Therefore was the name of it called Galeed and Mizpah; for he said,

The Lord watch between me and thee when we are absent one from another. If thou shalt afflict my daughters, or if thou shalt take other wives besides my daughters, no man is with us; see, God is witness between me and thee.

Behold this heap, and this pillar, they shall be witness that I will not pass this heap to thee, and that thou wilt not pass to me for harm.

The God of Abraham, and the God of Nahor, the God of their father, judge betwixt us. And Jacob sware by the Fear of his father Isaac.

Then Jacob offered a sacrifice upon the mount, and called his brethren to eat bread, and they did eat bread, and tarried all night in the mount.

And Laban rose up early in the morning, and kissed his sons and his daughters, and blessed them, and departed unto his place.

CONVERSATION XXI.

Mamma.—At what time did Jacob leave Haran?

Esther.—He fled whilst Laban had gone to shear his sheep.

Mamma.—Where did Laban overtake Jacob?

Esther.—Upon Mount Gilead.

Ada.—Do you think, dear Mamma, that Laban intended to do any harm to Jacob?

Mamma.—I do not think his intentions could have been peaceable, or we should not be told that God appeared to him, and commanded him not to do any harm to Jacob.

Esther.—Does it not appear very unkind of Jacob to have taken away Laban's daughters and his grandchildren, without having allowed them to bid Laban good-bye?

Mamma.—It certainly would seem so, but we may imagine that Jacob had good reason to believe that Laban would not have permitted him to go, had he made known his intentions whilst he was still in his power.

Esther.—Did Laban worship idols?

Mamma.—Laban appears to have believed in God, and yet his worship could not have been quite pure, or he would not have kept in his house the images which Rachel stole.

Ada.—If Rachel stole the images to prevent her father from worshipping them, do you think she did wrong?

Mamma.—My dear child, the act was wrong, whatever might have been the motive. In taking example from our Biblical characters, you must be careful not to confound motives with actions, and, as a rule for your own guidance, you may be sure that whenever you feel inclined to do a thing secretly, and hide it from your best friends, it is not right. Rachel did not let Jacob know that she had stolen the images; therefore, we may conclude that she did not consider her motive for doing so a right one. Now, Esther, tell me how did Jacob and Laban part?

Esther.—They made a covenant of peace, and set up a heap of stones as a witness between them.

Mamma.—What names did they give to the place where they entered into this covenant of peace?

Esther.—They called it גַּלְעֵד (Gal-ïd) and מִצְפָּה (Mitz-poh).

Mamma.—Give me the meanings of the two names?

Ada.—גַּלְעֵד (Gal-ïd) means witness and מִצְפָּה (Mitz-poh) watch tower. The place was called מִצְפָּה (Mitz-poh) because Laban said, "Let God watch between me and thee."

Mamma.—What was it Jacob did before Laban left him?

Esther.—He offered a sacrifice to God upon the mount, and eat bread with his brethren.

READING XXII.

———o———

And Jacob went on his way, and the angels of God met him, and when he saw them, he said, this is God's host.

And Jacob sent messengers before him to Esau his brother, unto the land of Seir, the country of Edom. And he commanded them, saying, Thus shall ye speak unto my lord Esau.

Thy servant Jacob saith thus; I have sojourned with Laban and stayed there until now. And I have oxen and asses, flocks, menservants, and womenservants, and I have sent to tell my lord that I may find grace in thy sight.

And the messengers returned to Jacob, saying, We came to thy brother Esau, and also he cometh to meet thee, and four hundred men with him.

Then Jacob was greatly afraid and distressed. And he divided the people that were with him, and the flocks, and the herds, and the camels, into two bands; and said, If Esau come to one company and smite it, then the other company which is left shall escape.

And Jacob said, O God of my father Isaac, the Lord which saidst unto me, Return into thy country and to thy kindred, and I will deal well with thee: I am not worthy of the least of all thy mercies, and of all the truth which thou hast shown to thy servant, for with my staff I passed over this Jordan and I am become two bands.

Deliver me, I pray Thee, from the hand of my

brother, from the hand of Esau; for I fear him lest he come and smite me, and the mothers with the children. And Thou saidst, I will surely do thee good, and make thy seed as the sand of the sea, which cannot be numbered for multitude.

And he lodged there that night, and took of that which came to his hand, a present for Esau his brother: two hundred she goats and twenty rams, thirty milch camels with their colts, forty kine, and ten bulls, twenty she asses, and ten foals.

And he delivered them into the hands of his servants, every drove by themselves, and said unto his servants, Pass over before me, and put a space between drove and drove.

And he commanded the foremost, saying, When Esau my brother meeteth thee and asketh thee, saying, Whose art thou? and whither goest thou? and whose are these before thee, then thou shalt say, They be thy servant Jacob's, sent as a present unto my lord Esau; and behold he is behind us.

And so commanded he the second, and the third, and all that followed the droves, saying, in this manner shall ye speak unto Esau when ye come to him. And say ye moreover, Behold, thy servant Jacob is behind us.

For he said, I will appease him with the present that goeth before me, and afterward I will see his face; perhaps he will accept of me.

So went the present over before him; and himself lodged that night in the company.

And Jacob rose up that night, and took his wives and his sons, and all that he had, and sent them over the ford Jabbok.

And being left alone, there wrestled a man with him until the breaking of the day. And when he saw that he prevailed not against him, he struck against the hollow of his thigh, and the hollow of

Jacob's thigh was put out of joint, as he wrestled with him.

And he said, Let me go, for the day breaketh. And he said, I will not let thee go, unless thou bless me.

And he said unto him, What is thy name? And he said, Jacob.

And he said, Thy name shall no more be called Jacob, but Israel; for as a prince hast thou power with God and with men, and hast prevailed.

And Jacob asked him, and said, Tell me, I pray thee, thy name. And he said, Wherefore is it that thou dost ask after my name? And he blessed him there.

And Jacob called the name of the place Peniel, for I have seen an angel of God face to face, and my life is preserved.

And as he passed over Peniel, the sun rose upon him. And he halted upon his thigh.

Therefore the children of Israel eat not of the sinew which shrank, which is upon the hollow of the thigh, unto this day.

CONVERSATION XXII.

Mamma.—Name the place to which Jacob sent messengers?

Esther.—Jacob sent messengers before him to Edom, to his brother Esau.

Mamma.—For what purpose did Jacob send these messengers before him?

Ada.—To conciliate his brother, and to let him know of his return to his own land.

Mamma.—When Esau returned no answer by Jacob's messenger, how did Jacob feel?

Esther.—He felt afraid and distressed. Did he think that Esau was coming to kill him?

Mamma.—It was not unlikely that he should think so, for you must remember Jacob had left home to avoid his brother's anger, and that he was conscious of having done him a great wrong.

Esther.—Do you think, Mamma, that Esau did intend to kill Jacob?

Mamma.—We will hope not; whenever we are uncertain of people's motives, we should always think that they mean well. We find afterwards, that Esau forgave his brother most generously, and did not even wish to take his present. What are we told of Jacob after his messengers had returned?

Ada.—That he prayed to God to deliver him from the hand of his brother.

Mamma.—Have you remarked how the words of this prayer of Jacob's show his sincere repentance for the acts of his youth, his acknowledgment of his own unworthiness, and his entire reliance upon God?

Ada.—I do not feel quite convinced that he shewed his

entire reliance upon God, for did he not afterwards take every precaution for his safety, and the safety of his cattle, his wives, and his children?

Mamma.—My dear child, you have fallen into a very common error, in imagining that God will grant our prayers if we make no efforts ourselves; it is true, that nothing is beyond the power of the Almighty, but He has gifted man with intelligence, and we are plainly shown throughout our Bible, that it is proper to use that intelligence as well as every means within our power, to accomplish all that is right. When we say we have faith in God, we do not mean that we are to sit still and expect Him to shower His blessings upon us; but that we believe (that having done all that is possible ourselves) God will direct the events of our lives, for our own good and the good of our fellow-creatures.

Ada.—Does it not appear strange that Jacob should have prevailed over the angel of God?

Mamma.—My dear child, there is much in this passage which it is not easy to understand; some of our commentators have derived a beautiful moral lesson from this event of Jacob's life; but the discussion of this passage is too difficult for my little Esther at present, and I think even you had better defer it till you are older.

Ada.—Mamma, we are told that the children of Israel eat not of the sinew that shrank unto this day, because the angel touched the hollow of Jacob's thigh and it shrank. I believe that is the reason we do not now eat of the leg of the animal until it has been porged, but this is not a command. Do you think there is any harm if we eat of it?

Mamma.—On this I must give you my own opinion, as I have had no means of studying what our Rabbis have said on the subject. I think if our lawgiver, Moses, had considered this custom unnecessary, at the same time that he told us of it, he would have said, we need observe it no longer; and my own idea is, unless we find that our customs are observed from wrong or superstitious motives, and evidently against the laws of Moses, it is better to observe them, even though they are *not* actual commands.

Esther.—Mamma, dear, are we called Israelites because God changed Jacob's name from Jacob to Israel?

Mamma.—Yes, my dear; since you have asked this question, I suppose you can tell me the meaning of the name?

Esther.—God gave Jacob this name because the angel said, "As a prince hast thou power with God and men, and hast prevailed." יִשְׂרָאֵל (Yi'sroïl) means to wrestle with God.

Mamma.—What name did Jacob give the place where he had wrestled with the angel?

Esther.—He called it פְּנִיאֵל (Pene-ïl), which means face of God, for he said, I have seen God face to face.

Ada.—But, Mamma, this could not have been true, for God said to Moses, "No man can see my face and live."

Mamma.—Although in our English Bible we have the words rendered, "I have seen God face to face," I think we might more properly render פְּנִיאֵל (Pene-ïl)—presence of God. The terms *face* and *presence* are often synonymous even in English, and Jacob's interview with an angel, (or direct messenger from God) would naturally lead him to feel himself in the immediate presence of the Almighty.

Ada.—Do you think there was any reason that the angel refused to give his name to Jacob?

Mamma.—It appears most probable that the angel was forbidden by God to give himself a name, lest he might become in after ages an object of worship. You know we are strictly forbidden to offer prayers to, or to conceive the possibility of, any other being possessing power, but God Himself.

Esther.—What is an angel, Mamma?

Mamma.—I think I have told you before, that we do not know; human beings cannot know the nature of everything; there are many things which we see every day of which we understand but very little. The same Creator who formed ourselves, has formed millions of other beings. There is no limit to His power. And all that is necessary for us to know is, that whatever beings may exist, in whatever sphere they may dwell, all are equally subservient to God's will, and can neither benefit nor harm mankind but as His will directs.

READING XXIII.

And Jacob lifted up his eyes and looked, and beheld Esau coming, and with him four hundred men.

And he divided the children unto Leah, and unto Rachel, and to the two handmaidens. And he put the handmaids and their children foremost, and Leah and her children after, and Rachel and Joseph hindermost.

And he passed over before them, and bowed himself to the ground seven times, until he came near to his brother.

And Esau ran to meet him, and embraced him, and fell on his neck, and kissed him and wept.

And he lifted up his eyes and saw the women and the children, and said, Who are those with thee? And Jacob said, The children which God hath been pleased to give thy servant.

Then the handmaids came near with their children, and they bowed themselves. And Leah and her children came near and bowed themselves. And after came Rachel and Joseph near, and bowed themselves.

And Esau said, What meanest thou by all this drove which I met?

And Jacob said, These are to find grace in the sight of my lord.

And Esau said, I have enough, my brother; keep unto thyself what thou hast.

And Jacob said, Nay, I pray thee, if now I have found grace in thy sight, then receive the present at my hand; for I have seen thy face, as though I had seen the face of God, and thou wast pleased with me.

Take, I pray thee, my blessing that is brought to thee, because God hath dealt kindly with me, and because I have enough. And he urged him, and he took it.

And Esau said unto him, Let us take our journey, and I will go before thee.

And Jacob said, My lord knoweth that the children are tender, and the flocks and the herds with their young are with me. And if they should overdrive them they may die.

Let my lord pass over before his servant; and I will lead on slowly, as the cattle and the children are able to endure, until I come unto my lord unto Mount Seir.

And Esau said, Let me now leave with thee some of the people that are with me.

So Esau returned that day unto Seir; and Jacob journeyed to Succoth, and built him an house, and made booths for his cattle.

And he came to Shalem, a city of Shechem, which is in the land of Canaan, and pitched his tent before the city. And he erected there an altar before the Lord.

And God said unto Jacob, Arise, go up to Bethel, and dwell there; and make there an altar unto God, that appeared unto thee when thou fleddest from the face of Esau thy brother.

Then Jacob said unto his household, and to all that were with him, Put away the strange gods that are among you, and be clean, and change your garments; and let us arise and go to Bethel, and I will make there an altar unto God, who answered me in the day of my distress, and was with me in the way which I went.

And they gave unto Jacob all the strange gods

which were in their hands, and all the earrings which were in their ears ; and Jacob hid them under the oak which was by Shechem.

And they journeyed and came to Luz, which is in the land of Canaan. And Deborah, Rebekah's nurse, died, and she was buried beneath Bethel, under an oak.

And God appeared unto Jacob again, and said unto him, I am God Almighty, be fruitful and multiply. A nation and a multitude of nations shall come from thee, and the land which I gave Abraham and Isaac, to thee will I give it, and to thy seed after thee.

And God went up from him, in the place he talked with him.

And Jacob set up a pillar of stone there, and he poured a drink offering and oil thereon. And Jacob called the name of the place where God met him, Bethel (House of God).

And they journeyed towards Ephrath ; and Rachel bare a son and then died ; and when Rachel knew that she should die, she called her son Benoni, but Jacob called his name Benjamin.

And Rachel was buried in the way to Ephrath, which is Bethlehem. And Jacob set a pillar upon Rachel's grave. And Israel journeyed and spread his tent beyond the town Edar.

And he came unto Isaac, his father, unto Mamre.

And Isaac gave up the ghost and died, and was gathered unto his people, being old and full of days, and his sons, Esau and Jacob, buried him.

And the days of Isaac were an hundred and fourscore years.

And Esau took his wives, and his sons and daughters, and all the persons of his house; his cattle and beasts, and all his substance which he had got, in the land of Canaan, and went into the country from the face of his brother Jacob.

For their riches were so great that they could not dwell together; and the land could not bear them because of the cattle.

Then dwelt Esau in Mount Seir, and was the father of the Edomites in Mount Seir.

CONVERSATION XXIII.

Mamma.—How did Jacob and Esau meet?

Esther.—Esau ran towards his brother and embraced him, and fell on his neck and wept.

Mamma.—How did Jacob answer when Esau asked him concerning the women and the children whom he saw with him?

Esther.—Jacob said, " These are the children which God hath been pleased to give thy servant."

Ada.—When Jacob addresses Esau as my lord and calls himself his servant, do you think, Mamma, that he meant to acknowledge Esau's superiority over himself?

Mamma.—I should fancy that was not exactly his intention; the words " thy servant and my lord" appear to me to be used only as forms of courtesy, in the same manner as we often in the present day subscribe ourselves in a letter as " Your humble servant" to a person to whom we have no idea of submitting in such a capacity. How did Esau answer Jacob when the latter told him the droves he had were intended as a present to him?

Esther.—He said, " I have enough, my brother; keep what thou hast to thyself."

Mamma.—Did Esau at last accept the present?

Esther.—Yes; Jacob urged him, and he took it.

Ada.—Mamma, why do you think Jacob was so anxious that Esau should accept his present?

Mamma.—As a sign that he had quite forgiven his past conduct towards him, for it was even in the days of Jacob and Esau as it would be now. A person would not accept a present from one with whom he did not wish to be upon friendly terms; and it appears that Esau only accepted the present as an assurance of his good feeling towards Jacob, for he had freely forgiven him when they first met. Did Jacob accompany his brother Esau?

Esther.—No; he promised to follow him, for he said the women, children, and young cattle could not travel as fast as his brother and the men.

Mamma.—Where did Jacob next encamp?

Esther.—At Succoth.

Mamma.—Why was this place so called?

Ada.—Because Jacob made there tents or booths for his cattle.

Mamma.—What did Jacob require of all the people who were with him, before he should go to Bethel, where he intended to erect an altar unto God?

Esther.—That they should put away the strange gods that were among them, and change their garments and be clean.

Mamma.—Have you noticed that the words "*to be clean*" appear in this passage to bear a double meaning, that is, a figurative as well as a literal one; the people were "to put away the images," thus cleansing their hearts from impure worship, and "to change their garments" so as to prepare their bodies to enter the presence of God.

Ada.—Do you think that our prayers will not be equally acceptable to God whatever clothing we have on?

Mamma.—I do not think, or mean you for a moment to suppose, that God has regard to our garments, whether they be rich or poor, when we address him in prayer; but throughout the whole of our law the strictest cleanliness of person is enjoined. We can only show other people that we honour and reverence our Creator, by our outward demeanour. Our neatness and cleanliness prove, that we do not offer our prayers to God in an off-hand and slovenly manner.

Esther.—It seems very strange that Jacob should have taken the people's earrings and have buried them with the strange gods under the oak.

Mamma.—It would seem a very strange proceeding, if the mention of these earrings at the same time with the other images, did not lead us to believe that engraven upon these earrings were the likenesses of some idols which Jacob feared his servants might fall into the error of worshipping. It is possible that some of the people still retained idolatrous worship which Jacob was anxious to eradicate. Who died at Bethel?

Esther.—Deborah, Rebekah's nurse.

Mamma.—How did God at this time signify His approval of Jacob's actions?

Ada.—By appearing to him and repeating the promise He had made to Abraham, that Jacob's seed should possess the land.

Mamma.—What happened as Jacob and his family journeyed?

Esther.—Benjamin was born, and Rachel died.

Mamma.—Can you tell me the two names given to Benjamin, and their meanings?

Ada.—Rachel, when she knew that she would die, called her son Benoni, בֶּן־אוֹנִי (Ben-owné), son of my sorrow, but Jacob called him Benjamin, בִּנְיָמִין (Ben-yomin), son of my right hand.

Mamma.—Of what event do we read next?

Esther.—Of Isaac's death. What is the meaning, Mamma, of the words "Gave up the ghost?"

Mamma.—Ghost means spirit, my dear child. We understand this to mean that the spirit was parted from the body, and that the body consequently died. We have here again a proof, from the very form of speech, that the Israelites in all ages believed the soul which animates our bodies to be immortal.

Esther.—You mean by this that the soul still lives when we are dead. Where does it go, then, dear Mamma?

Mamma.—This is more than I can tell you, my darling. God has not revealed to us His method of dealing with our souls. We may feel sure that He has in store for us rewards or punishments according to the deserts of our actions in life. We should neither be the happier nor the better for knowing their exact nature; all that we should think of the future for, is, that it may induce us to act according to our best abilities here in this life, and having done all that lies in our power, we may rest content and trust that God will bless our efforts for good, and deal mercifully with our faults, for we know that He has pronounced Himself as a God of mercy, as well as of justice.

Ada.—Do you mean to say, Mamma, that it is wrong to think of what will happen to us after our death?

Mamma.—I mean to say, my darling, that it is useless to trouble ourselves with thoughts upon subjects which it is impossible for us to understand. All that is within our reach, and proper for us to know, cannot be learned even in a long lifetime.

Ada.—And yet you say we ought to try to learn all we can.

Mamma.—Yes, my dear child, and we should never let a day of our lives pass without endeavouring to acquire something that will make us wiser and better than we were the day before. Now, tell me, where Esau dwelt when he again separated from Jacob, because the land could not bear the cattle of both of them? And then we shall have had conversation enough for to-day.

Esther.—Esau dwelt in Mount Seir, and was the father of the Edomites.

READING XXIV.

And Jacob dwelt in the land of Canaan.

And Joseph, the son of Rachel, being seventeen years old, was feeding the flock with his brethren; and the lad was with the sons of Bilhah and the sons of Zilpah, and Joseph brought unto their father their evil report.

Now Israel loved Joseph more than all his children, and he made him a coat of many colours.

And when his brethren saw that their father loved him more than themselves, they hated him, and would not speak peaceably unto him.

And Joseph dreamed a dream, and told it to his brethren, and they hated him yet more.

And he said, Hear I pray you this dream which I have dreamed; for behold, we were binding sheaves in the field, and lo, my sheaf arose, and stood upright; and behold, your sheaves stood round about, and made obeisance to my sheaf.

And his brethren said, Shalt thou indeed reign over us, and shalt thou indeed have dominion over us? and they hated him yet more for these words and for his dreams.

And he dreamed yet another dream, and told it to his brethren, and said, Behold the sun, moon, and the eleven stars made obeisance to me.

And he told it to his father and to his brethren, and his father rebuked him, saying, Shall I and thy mother, and thy brethren, indeed come to bow down ourselves to thee?

And his brethren envied him, but his father observed the saying.

And his brethren went to feed their father's flock in Shechem.

And Israel said unto Joseph, Come, and I will send thee unto thy brethren, and he said, Here am I.

And Jacob said unto Joseph, Go, I pray thee, see whether it be well with thy brethren, and well with the flocks, and bring me word again. So he sent him out of the vale of Hebron and he came to Shechem.

And a certain man found him, and behold he was wandering in the field. And the man said, What seekest thou? And he said, I seek my brethren: tell me, I pray thee, where they feed their flocks? and the man said, They are departed hence, for I heard them say, Let us go to Dothan.

And Joseph went after his brethren, and found them in Dothan.

And when they saw him afar off, even before he came near unto them, they conspired against him to slay him.

And they said one to another, Behold, this dreamer cometh. Come now, therefore, let us slay him, and cast him into some pit; and we will say some evil beast hath devoured him, and we shall see what will become of his dreams.

And Reuben heard it, and said, Let us not kill him; shed no blood; but cast him into this pit that is in the wilderness, and lay no hand upon him:— that he might rid him out of their hands, and deliver him to his father again.

And it came to pass, that when Joseph was come unto his brethren, that they stripped off his coat of many colours that was on him. And they took and cast him into a pit which was empty.

And they sat down to eat bread, and they beheld a company of Ishmaelites coming from Gilead with their camels bearing spicery, and balm, and myrrh, going to carry it down to Egypt.

And Judah said unto his brethren, What profit is it if we slay our brother, and conceal his blood? Come, let us sell him to the Ishmaelites, and let not our hand be upon our brother and our flesh, and they agreed.

Then they drew and lifted up Joseph out of the pit, and sold him for twenty pieces of silver, and they took Joseph into Egypt.

And Reuben, being absent, knew not what was done, and returning unto the pit, beheld that Joseph was not there.

And he rent his clothes and went unto his brethren and said, The child is not, and I, whither shall I go?

And they killed a kid, and took Joseph's coat and dipped it in the blood, and brought it unto their father, and said, This have we found; know now whether it be thy son's coat or no.

And he knew it, and said, It is my son's coat; an evil beast hath devoured him. Joseph is without doubt torn in pieces.

And Jacob rent his clothes, and put sackcloth upon his loins, and mourned for his son many days.

And all his sons and his daughters rose up to comfort him; but he refused to be comforted, and he said, I will go down into the grave unto my son mourning.

Thus his father wept for him.

CONVERSATION XXIV.

Mamma.—What was the cause of Joseph's brothers' dislike to him?

Esther.—The evil report which Joseph brought his father of them.

Ada.—Do you not think it was wrong of Joseph to tell his father of the faults of his brothers?

Mamma.—I do not think it was right; we should never talk about the faults of others, if we can possibly avoid doing so.

Esther.—But, Mamma, ought we to let other people do wrong if we know it?

Mamma.—No, we should endeavour, if possible, to make them do right, by representing to them gently that we believe them to be in error, but we do no good by speaking of their faults to others, and it is wrong to make mischief. Further on in the Bible (after the law was given) there is an express command from God not to " go up and down as a tale-bearer among our people." You may perceive in the example before us, the only effect of Joseph's conduct was to excite the hatred of his brethren.

Ada.—Was it right of Jacob to love Joseph better than his other children?

Mamma.—It was not right of him to *show* his preference, and if you think of Joseph's history, you will perceive how severely Jacob suffered in consequence of having indulged this feeling. Perhaps it was not right of Jacob to make Joseph a particularly handsome coat, thus showing that he preferred him to his brethren; but he could not help loving him better, for it appears that he was a more dutiful child, and he was also the son of Jacob's favourite wife, Rachel, who died while Joseph was yet young.

Esther.—Do you think, dear Mamma, that a coat of many colours could have been particularly pretty?

Mamma.—Yes, my dear, it is possible that this coat was nicely embroidered. We do not fancy that this coat was made of different pieces of stuff. Now, can you tell me Joseph's dreams, and the reason that his brothers hated him more on account of them?

Esther.—He first dreamed "that he was binding sheaves with his brothers in the field, and that his sheaf stood upright, while those of his brothers bowed down to it;" then again "he dreamed that the sun, moon and eleven stars came and made obeisance to him."

Mamma.—Well, and how did the brothers interpret these dreams?

Esther.—They thought that Joseph wished to show them that he would rule over them.

Mamma.—Can you tell me, Ada, if these dreams were really prophetical?

Ada.—Yes, Mamma, and the prophecy was fulfilled when Joseph's brethren came down to buy corn of him in Egypt.

Mamma.—What did Joseph's brethren say when they saw him coming towards them?

Esther.—They agreed to kill him, saying, "We shall see what will become of his dreams."

Mamma.—Did all Joseph's brothers conspire against him?

Ada—No; Reuben tried to save him, by telling the other brothers to cast him into a pit, whence he thought to remove him and deliver him to his father again.

Esther.—How was it that Reuben allowed his brothers to sell Joseph to the Ishmaelites?

Mamma.—Reuben must have been away from his brothers at the time of the arrival of the Ishmaelites. Do you not remember his lamentation when he returned to the pit and found it empty.

Ada.—I remember, Mamma, Reuben rent his clothes and said, "The child is not, and I, whither shall I go?"

Esther.—Did not Reuben help to deceive his father by taking him the coat dipped in blood?

Mamma.—It is possible, and appears most probable, that

Reuben was himself deceived: if he did not believe, as Jacob did, that Joseph had been torn in pieces by some wild animal, he might have thought that he had been murdered by his brethren, and it would have been useless to have told his father of his suspicions.

Esther.—Why did Jacob tear his clothes when he heard of Joseph's death?

Mamma.—This was the method in which the people of eastern nations showed their grief; to us it appears strange, because English people, either in joy or sorrow, are very undemonstrative; that is to say, they exhibit very few signs of joy or sorrow, whilst people in other countries will commonly tear their hair or their clothes, and utter the wildest shrieks and lamentations, to display their grief; in the same way they will dance about and clap their hands for joy. We, at the present day have our dresses torn at the death of a near relative, and wear the torn garment during the month; this, like many of our other customs, is a remnant of our eastern origin. Now tell me, Esther, to whom did Joseph's brethren sell him?

Esther.—To some Ishmaelitish merchants who were going into Egypt with balm, myrrh, and spices.

Mamma.—What did Jacob say when his sons and daughters endeavoured to comfort him?

Esther.—He said, " I will go down into the grave unto my son mourning."

READING XXV.

And the Midianites sold Joseph into Egypt unto Potiphar, an officer of Pharaoh, and captain of the guard; and the Lord was with Joseph, and prospered him, and he was in the house of his master the Egyptian.

And Joseph found grace in his sight, and he made him overseer over his house, and all that he had he put into his hand; and the Lord blessed the Egyptian's house, for Joseph's sake.

And Joseph was a goodly person, and well-favoured.

And it came to pass after these things, that his master's wife tempted Joseph, and wished him to do evil, but he refused, and said,

How can I do this great wickedness, and sin against God?

Then her heart was filled with enmity against Joseph, because he would not sin. And she complained of him to her husband, and lied against him.

And it came to pass, when his master heard the words of his wife, saying, After this manner did thy servant unto me, that his wrath was kindled, and he took Joseph and he put him into prison, a place where the king's prisoners were bound.

But the Lord was with Joseph and showed him mercy, and gave him favour in the sight of the keeper of the prison, who committed into Joseph's hand all the other prisoners.

And the keeper of the prison looked not to anything that was under his hand, because the Lord was with Joseph, and made all that he did to prosper.

And it came to pass that the chief butler and the chief baker of the King of Egypt had offended their lord, and Pharaoh was wroth against them, and put them into the prison where Joseph was confined. And the captain of the guard charged Joseph with them.

And they each dreamed a dream in one night, and when Joseph came in to them in the morning, he beheld them both sad, and said, Wherefore look ye so sadly to-day?

And they said, We have each dreamed a dream, and there is no one to interpret it.

And Joseph said, Do not interpretations belong to God? tell me them, I pray you.

And the chief butler said, In my dream, behold a vine was before me, and on the vine were three branches: and it was as though it budded, and her blossoms shot forth; and the clusters brought forth ripe grapes; and Pharaoh's cup was in my hand. And I took the grapes, and pressed them into Pharaoh's cup, and gave the cup into Pharaoh's hand.

And Joseph said unto him, The three branches are three days. Within three days shall Pharaoh lift up thine head, and restore thee unto thy place: and thou shalt deliver Pharaoh's cup into his hand, after the former manner, when thou wast his butler.

But think on me, when it shall be well with thee, and show kindness unto me, I pray thee, and make mention of me unto Pharaoh, and bring me out of this house: for, indeed, I was stolen away out of the land of the Hebrews: and here also have I done nothing that they should put me into the dungeon.

Then the chief baker said unto Joseph, I also, in my dream, had three white baskets on my head, and in the uppermost basket there were all manner of baked meats for Pharaoh; and the birds did eat them out of the basket upon my head.

And Joseph said, The three baskets are three days: within three days Pharaoh shall lift up thy head, and shall hang thee on a tree; and the birds shall eat up thy flesh from off thee.

And it came to pass on the third day, which was Pharaoh's birthday, that he made a feast unto all his servants, and he lifted up the head of the chief butler, and of the chief baker among his servants.

And he restored the chief butler again unto his butlership, and he gave the cup into Pharaoh's hand. But he hanged the chief baker, as Joseph had said to them.

Yet did not the chief butler remember Joseph, but forgat him.

CONVERSATION XXV.

Mamma.—To whom did the Midianites sell Joseph?

Esther.—To Potiphar, an officer of Pharaoh and captain of the guard.

Mamma.—What do we read next of Joseph?

Esther.—That God was with him, and blessed the Egyptian's house for Joseph's sake.

Mamma.—Did Potiphar treat Joseph kindly?

Esther.—Yes, he trusted him entirely, and made him overseer over his house.

Mamma.—Why did Potiphar's wife complain of Joseph to her husband, and cause him to be thrown into prison?

Esther.—Because she tempted him to sin, and he refused.

Mamma.—How was Joseph treated in the prison?

Esther.—He gained favour in the sight of the keeper of the prison, and all the other prisoners were committed into Joseph's hand.

Mamma.—What remarkable personages were imprisoned at the same time with Joseph?

Esther.—The chief butler and the chief baker of Pharaoh.

Mamma.—What do we read of them?

Esther.—That they each dreamed a dream which troubled them, and that when Joseph came to them in the morning he beheld them both sad.

Mamma.—What did he say to them?

Esther.—He offered to interpret their dreams.

Mamma.—Can you remember his words?

Ada.—He said, "Do not interpretations belong to God? Tell them to me, I pray you."

Mamma.—What did Joseph mean them to understand by these words?

Esther.—That God had given him the power to interpret their dreams.

Mamma.—Quite right, my dear child; he wished them clearly to understand, that his interpretations could only be given, according to the inspiration which he received from God.

Ada.—Mamma, dear, you have often said to us that it is wrong to attach any importance to our dreams, yet we find throughout the Bible many instances where God sent dreams as prophecies.

Mamma.—If God were to send us dreams that foretold any events in which we were to act, or if He sent us an interpretation and the event came to pass, as these events which we find related in the Bible did, we should believe now even as people did then; but when I caution you against believing in dreams, I am only teaching you obedience to a precept expressly given in our תּוֹרָה ('Tou-rah)—which we shall read by-and-bye—where we are told not to believe in signs or omens, or to listen to the words of a prophet, unless something of which he tells us comes to pass. In all ages there have been false prophets and people who superstitiously attach importance to particular dreams, making these dreams indicate things which are to occur, thus giving themselves much unhappiness and many needless disappointments.

Esther.—You mean, Mamma, that it is wrong to believe as the servants tell us sometimes, that our dream is a sign of a fire or a wedding or of hasty news.

Mamma.—Exactly, my dear; all these things are wrong. All that we have to do is to act always to the best of our abilities, and then trust events to God, without troubling ourselves as to what may happen; but now let us finish with the dreams of the butler and baker. Tell me the results of Joseph's interpretation?

Esther.—The chief baker was to be hanged, and the chief butler restored to his place within three days.

Mamma.—What request did Joseph make of the chief butler when these things should come to pass?

Esther.—That he would remember him and intercede with Pharaoh for his release from prison.

Mamma.—Did the butler do so?

Esther.—No; he forgot him.

READING XXVI.

And it came to pass, at the end of two full years, that Pharaoh dreamed; and, behold, he stood by the river.

And, behold, there came out of the river seven well-favoured kine, and fat-fleshed, and they fed in a meadow; and, behold, seven kine came up after them out of the river, ill-favoured, and lean-fleshed, and stood by the other kine, upon the brink of the river.

And the ill-favoured and lean-fleshed kine did eat up the seven well-favoured and fat kine: and Pharaoh awoke.

And he slept and dreamed a second time; and, behold, seven ears of corn came up upon one stalk, rank and good. And, behold, seven thin ears, and blasted with the east wind, sprung up after them; and the seven thin ears devoured the seven rank and full ears.

Then Pharaoh awoke, and, behold, it was a dream.

And in the morning his spirit was troubled. And he called all the magicians of Egypt, and all the wise men thereof.

And Pharaoh told them his dreams, but there were none that could interpret them unto Pharaoh.

Then said the chief butler, I do remember my faults this day: and he told Pharaoh his dream, and the dream of the chief baker, and how Joseph did interpret them, as it came to pass.

Then Pharaoh sent and called Joseph hastily out of the dungeon: and he shaved himself and changed his raiment, and came and stood before Pharaoh.

And Pharaoh told his dream unto Joseph, and said, I have heard of thee, that thou canst understand a dream to interpret it.

And Joseph answered Pharaoh, saying, It is not in me: God shall give Pharaoh an answer of peace.

And Joseph said, The dream of Pharaoh is one. God hath showed Pharaoh what He is about to do.

The seven good kine are seven years, and the seven good ears are seven years, and the seven thin and ill-favoured kine that came up after them are seven years, and the seven empty ears, blasted with the east wind, are seven years of famine.

This is the thing which I have spoken unto Pharaoh, What God is about to do, He hath shown unto Pharaoh.

Behold, there come seven years of great plenty throughout all the land of Egypt; and there shall arise after them seven years of famine; and the plenty shall not be known in the land by reason of the famine; for it shall be very grievous.

The dream was doubled unto Pharaoh, showing that the thing is certain, and God will shortly bring it to pass.

Now, therefore, let Pharaoh look out a man, wise and discreet, and set him over the land of Egypt, and let him appoint officers over the land, and take up the fifth part of the land, in the seven plenteous years.

And let them gather all the food of those good years that are to come, and let them lay up corn under the hand of Pharaoh, and let them keep food in the cities.

And that food shall be for store against the seven years of famine, which shall be in the land of Egypt, that the land perish not through the famine.

And the thing was good in the eyes of Pharaoh, and in the eyes of all his servants.

And Pharaoh said unto his servants, Can we find such a man as this is, a man in whom the spirit of God is?

And Pharaoh said unto Joseph, Forasmuch as God hath showed thee all this, there is none so discreet and wise as thou art.

Thou shalt be over my house, and according to thy word shall all my people be ruled: only on the throne will I be greater than thou.

And Pharaoh said unto Joseph, See, I have set thee over all the land of Egypt.

And Pharaoh took off his ring from his hand, and put it upon Joseph's hand, and arrayed him in vestures of fine linen, and put a gold chain about his neck.

And he made him to ride in the second chariot which he had: and they cried before him, Bow the knee. And he made him ruler over all the land of Egypt.

And Pharaoh said unto Joseph, I am Pharaoh, and without thee shall no man lift up the hand, or foot, in all the land of Egypt.

And Pharaoh gave Joseph to wife Asenath, daughter of the priest of On. And Pharaoh called Joseph Zaphnath-paaneah.

And Joseph went out over all the land of Egypt.

And Joseph was thirty years old when he stood before Pharaoh.

CONVERSATION XXVI.

Mamma.—How long did Joseph remain in prison after the release of the chief butler?

Esther.—Two years.

Mamma.—What happened at the end of this time that caused the chief butler to remember Joseph?

Esther.—Pharaoh's dreams, which he could find no one to interpret.

Mamma.—Can you relate to me these dreams?

Esther.—Yes, dear Mamma; "Pharaoh dreamed first that seven well-favoured kine came up out of the river, and that they were followed by seven lean kine which devoured them, and yet did not look any better; he then fell asleep again, and dreamed that seven ears of corn came up upon one stalk, rank and good; and after these followed seven thin ears, blasted with the east wind, and devoured the seven full ears."

Mamma.—Very well remembered, my darling. Now, tell me what Joseph said, when Pharaoh told him that he had heard that Joseph understood a dream to interpret it?

Esther.—He said, "It is not in me. God will give Pharaoh an answer of peace."

Mamma.—Have you thought of the lesson that these words of Joseph were meant to convey?

Ada.—You told us before, dear Mamma, when Joseph said almost the same thing to the chief butler and the chief baker, that he wished to show that it was to God that he owed the power of interpreting correctly.

Mamma.—Yes, my dear, undoubtedly Joseph's principal meaning was to show the magicians of Egypt that the gift of prophecy could be acquired by no human efforts; but I think we may also take another lesson from these words of Joseph, and apply it to any one who excels his fellow-creatures in any one quality—that is, that whatever gifts we may possess, whether of beauty, talent, wisdom or wealth, we should not, on account of them, think ourselves better than one less favoured, but acknowledge that these gifts are entrusted to us by God; that we should think humbly of ourselves, knowing that it is in the power of our Almighty Father to deprive us in an instant of any gift He may have bestowed.

Ada.—Mamma, do not Pharaoh's dreams appear very plainly to indicate the meaning given to them?

Mamma.—Yes, my dear, after we have been told what it was. When we read what is to happen, and see its fulfilment, we can very easily trace the symbols. Do not fall into the error of imagining, that because things appear easy when explained, that it required no special gift to explain them correctly. Since you have found the interpretation so plain, just relate to me the symbols given? and how they indicated most appropriately the coming events?

Ada.—Both the fat kine and the full ears being devoured by the lean ones, plainly indicated a famine so grievous that the land would be no better for the great plenty that had preceded it.

Mamma.—You have not thought of that part of the vision, which shows how the abundance or failure of the crops in Egypt was affected by the river Nile. Pharaoh saw both the kine and the ears come out of the Nile.

Esther.—I noticed this, Mamma; but what had the river to do with the plenty or the famine?

Mamma.—Simply this, my darling, which I could not expect you to know; but which I have no doubt this fact will cause you to remember—namely, that Egypt is a country where no rain falls, and that the soil is dependant for water upon the rise of the river, which overflows its banks annually, and, besides watering the ground, leaves a deposit which renders it fruitful. The Egyptians anxiously watch the rise of this river, for they know that their crops will be abundant or scarce in proportion as the waters rise or fall.

Ada.—I believe I have read of this, dear Mamma, but I did not think of the connection between the Nile and the crops, when considering the interpretation of Pharaoh's dream.

Mamma.—Now tell me, Esther, in as few words as possible, how were Pharaoh's dreams interpreted?

Esther.—Joseph told Pharaoh that they had been sent him by God, to show that there would come immediately in the land of Egypt seven years of great plenty, which were to be followed by seven years of grievous famine.

Mamma.—Do you remember the advice Joseph gave Pharaoh after having interpreted the dreams?

Esther.—Yes; he advised Pharaoh to choose a man who was discreet and wise, and to set him over the land of Egypt, to gather up stores during the years of plenty, so that the people might be saved alive during the years of famine that were to follow.

Mamma.—Did Pharaoh attend to this advice?

Esther.—Yes, and chose Joseph, and set him over the land of Egypt. Made him second only to the king, and gave him handsome presents of a ring and a chain, and robed him in fine vestments.

Mamma.—You have remembered correctly, but your idea of the presents is not quite clear: the ring and chain were not intended merely as presents, but as signs that the king had bestowed authority upon Joseph; the king's ring was without doubt the ring which bore his seal; and the king's seal attached to any document was regarded in those days as the Queen's signature would be in the present time; thus Pharaoh gave Joseph permission to issue any decree he pleased, and sign it, without first referring to him.

I wish you also to remark, that Joseph was not only the first Jewish Prime Minister that we have on record, but also the first in the world who held that situation. Israelites appear since then in the history of many countries as Ministers of Finance.

READING XXVII.

And Joseph went out from the presence of Pharaoh, and went over all the land of Egypt.

And in the seven plenteous years, the earth brought forth by handfuls.

And he gathered up all the food of the seven years, and laid it up in the cities: the food of the fields which were round about every city, laid he up in the same.

And Joseph gathered up corn as the sand of the sea.

And unto Joseph were born two sons, before the years of famine came; which Asenath bare unto him.

And Joseph called the name of the firstborn, Manasseh: For God, said he, hath made me forget all my toil of my father's house.

And the name of the second he called Ephraim; For God hath caused me to be fruitful in the land of my affliction.

And the seven years of plenty, that was in the land of Egypt, were ended.

And the seven years of dearth were come, as Joseph had said; and the dearth was in all the lands; but in the land of Egypt there was bread.

And when all the land of Egypt was famished the people cried to Pharaoh for bread, and Pharaoh said unto them, Go unto Joseph; what he saith unto you, do.

And the famine was sore in Egypt, and over all the face of the earth.

And Joseph opened all the storehouses, and sold corn to the Egyptians; and all countries came unto Egypt to buy corn.

And when Jacob knew that there was corn in Egypt, he said unto his sons, Why do ye look one upon another?

Behold, I have heard that there is corn in Egypt: get ye down thither, and buy food for us from thence, that we may live and not die.

And Joseph's ten brethren went down to buy corn in Egypt. But Benjamin, Joseph's brother, Jacob sent not with his brethren, lest mischief should befall him.

And the sons of Israel came to buy corn in Egypt; And they bowed themselves before Joseph with their faces to the earth.

And Joseph saw his brethren, and knew them, but he made himself strange unto them, and spake roughly unto them.

And he said unto them, Whence come ye? And they said, From the land of Canaan, to buy food.

And they knew not Joseph. And Joseph thought of the dreams that he had dreamed.

And he said unto them, Ye are spies; to see the nakedness of the land are ye come.

And they said unto him, Nay, my lord, but to buy food are we, thy servants, come. We are all one man's sons; we are true men; thy servants are no spies.

And Joseph answered, Nay, but to see the nakedness of the land are ye come.

And they said, Thy servants are twelve brethren, the sons of one man in the land of Canaan, and behold the youngest is this day with our father; and one is not.

And Joseph said unto them, Hereby shall ye be proved. By the life of Pharaoh, ye shall not go forth hence, except your youngest brother come hither.

Let one go and fetch him; and ye shall be kept in prison, that your words may be proved whether there be any truth in you.

And he put them all together in ward, three days.

And on the third day Joseph said unto them, This do, and ye shall live, for I fear God; if ye be true men, let one of you be bound in prison, then go ye, take corn for your households, and bring your youngest brother unto me, so shall your words be proved and ye shall not die. And they did so.

And they said one to another, We are verily guilty concerning our brother, in that we saw not the anguish of his soul when he besought us and we would not hear; therefore is this distress come upon us.

And Reuben answered them, Spake I not unto you, saying, Do not sin against the child; and ye would not hear: therefore, behold his blood is required.

And they knew not that Joseph understood them, for when he spake to them, he had one with him to interpret.

And he turned from them and wept; and returned to them again, and spoke with them, and took from them Simeon, and bound him before their eyes.

Then Joseph commanded to fill their sacks with corn, and to restore every man's money into his sack, and to give them provision for the way. And thus did he unto them.

And they loaded their asses with corn and departed.

And as one of them opened his sack to give his ass provender in the inn, he espied his money; for behold it was in the sack's mouth.

And he said unto his brethren, My money is restored, and lo, it is even in my sack.

And their hearts failed them, and they were afraid,.

saying one to another, What is this that God hath done unto us?

And they came to Jacob their father, unto the land of Canaan, and told him all that had befallen them, saying,

The man who is lord of the land spake roughly unto us, and took us for spies.

And we said unto him, We are true men, we are no spies; we be twelve brethren, sons of one father; one is not; and the youngest is with our father this day, in the land of Canaan.

And the man, the lord of the country, said, Hereby shall I know that ye are true men: leave one of your brethren with me, and take food for your households and be gone: and bring your youngest brother unto me, then shall I know that ye are no spies, but that ye are true men; so will I deliver you your brother, and ye shall traffic in the land.

And it came to pass, as they emptied their sacks, that behold every man's money was in his sack.

And when they and their father saw the bundles of money they were afraid.

And Jacob their father said unto them, Me have ye bereaved of my children; Joseph is not, and Simeon is not; and ye will take Benjamin also. All these things are against me.

And Reuben said, Slay my two sons if I bring him not to thee; deliver him into my hand, and I will bring him to thee again.

And he said, My son shall not go down with you, for his brother is dead, and he is left alone;

If mischief befall him by the way then shall ye bring down my grey hairs with sorrow to the grave.

CONVERSATION XXVII.

Mamma.—When were Joseph's two sons born?

Esther.—Before the years of the famine.

Mamma.—What names did he give them? and what are the meanings of the names?

Esther.—Joseph called the firstborn, Manasseh, and the second Ephraim; מְנַשֶּׁה (Menasseh)—which means to cause to forget, for, said he, "God hath made me forget my toil in my father's house;" and אֶפְרָיִם (Ephraim)—means to be fruitful, for he said, "God hath made me fruitful in the land of my affliction."

Mamma.—Again, you notice that nearly all the names we read of in the Bible were given in commemoration of some event, or with some special signification?

Esther.—Yes, dear Mamma; so if we learn the signification, we can remember the events and the circumstances in which the people were placed.

Mamma.—Was Egypt the only country which suffered from the famine?

Esther.—No, all the surrounding countries, and amongst them Canaan, suffered likewise.

Mamma.—What is the next event we read of as occurring in consequence of the famine in Canaan?

Esther.—Joseph's brothers went into Egypt to buy food.

Mamma.—Which of Joseph's brothers remained at home with his father?

Esther.—Benjamin.

Mamma.—Did Joseph recognize his brethren?

Esther.—Yes; but they did not know him.

Mamma.—How did he receive them?

Esther.—He spake roughly to them, saying, "Ye are spies, and to see the nakedness of the land are ye come."

Mamma.—What did he desire them to do, to prove that they were true men?

Esther.—He told them to bring their younger brother, and he kept Simeon in prison.

Ada.—Do you not think, dear Mamma, that Joseph treated his brethren very unkindly and revengefully?

Mamma.—It would certainly seem so, if we did not perceive that it was another motive, and not one of revenge which prompted Joseph to pursue this line of conduct. It has always appeared to me that Joseph wished to find out whether his brethren had repented of the way in which they had treated him, and whether they might be trusted, and would not become jealous of any favors he might shew to Benjamin.

Ada.—Then, Mamma, he succeeded in his desires, for when he heard his brethren say that this trouble had come upon them on account of the way they had treated him, he must have been satisfied that they had repented.

Esther.—Why then, Mamma, did not Joseph make himself known to his brethren, before he sent them back to their father?

Mamma.—I cannot pretend to tell you with certainty, the motives which actuated him. We are often incorrect in our ideas of the motives and of the actions of our dearest friends, but if we consider the manner in which Joseph acted afterwards, it would appear that he only wished to be quite certain that he could trust them to live in peace and unity before he invited them into Egypt.

Esther.—I do not quite understand how it was that Joseph knew what his brothers were saying, and that they did not know that he did so.

Ada.—Do you not remember, Esther, that he spoke to them through an interpreter?

Mamma.—You have not helped Esther, my dear Ada, to understand this any better. My little girl does not know the meaning of the word interpreter. An interpreter is a person who understands the different languages in which two parties are speaking, and translates from one into the other: thus Joseph spoke in the language of Egypt, and the interpreter repeated his words in Hebrew to his brethren, whilst theirs which were spoken in Hebrew, he put again into the Egyptian.

Esther.— Thank you, dear Mamma; I understand this quite well now.

Mamma.—What did Joseph command his steward to do with the money his brethren had brought to buy corn?

Esther.—He desired that it should be returned in their sacks.

Mamma.—What were their feelings when they discovered it?

Esther.—They were afraid.

Mamma.—Did Jacob readily consent to let Benjamin accompany his brothers into Egypt, after he had been told what had occurred?

Esther.—No; he said, "Me have ye bereaved of my children: Joseph is not, and Simeon is not, and ye will take away Benjamin also."

Mamma.—Which of the brothers entreated Jacob to let Benjamin accompany them, offering to become surety for his safe return?

Esther.—Reuben, who said, "Slay my two sons if I bring him not again unto thee."

Mamma.—Did Jacob then consent that he should go with them?

Esther.—No: he said, "If mischief befall him, ye shall bring down my grey hairs with sorrow to the grave."

READING XXVIII.

———o———

AND the famine was sore in the land.

And it came to pass that when they had eaten up the corn which they had brought from Egypt, their father said unto them, Go again, and buy us a little food.

And Judah spake unto him, saying, The man did solemnly protest unto us, saying, Ye shall not see my face, except your brother be with you.

If thou wilt send our brother with us, we will go down and buy thee food; but if thou wilt not send him, we will not go down ; for the man said unto us, Ye shall see my face no more, except your brother be with you.

And Israel said, Wherefore dealt ye so ill with me, as to tell the man whether ye had yet a brother?

And they said, The man asked us straitly of our state, and of our kindred, saying, Is your father yet alive? Have ye another brother?

And we told him according to these words. Could we certainly know that he would say, Bring your brother down?

And Judah said to Israel his father, Send the lad with me, and we will arise and go ; that we may live and not die, both we, and thou, and also our little ones.

I will be surety for him; of my hand shalt thou require him; if I bring him not unto thee, and set him before thee, then let me bear the blame for ever.

And their father Israel said unto them, If it must

be so, now do this:—Take the best fruits in the land in your vessels, and carry down a present, a little balm, and a little honey, spices and myrrh, nuts and almonds.

And take double money in your hand; and the money that was brought back in your sacks carry it again in your hand.

Take also your brother, and arise and go again unto the man.

And God Almighty give you mercy before him, that he may send away your other brother and Benjamin.

If I am bereaved of my children, I am bereaved!

And the men took the presents, and the double money, and Benjamin, and went down to Egypt, and stood before Joseph.

And when Joseph saw Benjamin with them he said to the ruler of his house,

Bring these men home, and stay and make ready; for they shall dine with me at noon. And the man did as Joseph bade him, and brought the men into Joseph's house.

And they were afraid because they were brought unto Joseph's house, and they said, Because of the money that was returned in our sacks the first time are we brought in, that he may find occasion against us, and fall upon us, and take us for bondmen, together with our asses.

And they came near to the steward of Joseph's house, and spake with him at the door of the house,

And said, O sir! we came down indeed the first time to buy food. And it came to pass, when we got to the inn, that we opened our sacks, and behold, every man's money was in his sack.

And we have brought it back again; and money have we brought to buy food: we cannot tell who put the money in our sacks.

And he said, Peace be unto you; fear not. Your God and the God of your father hath given you treasure in your sacks. I had your money. And he brought Simeon out to them.

And the steward brought the men into Joseph's house, and gave them water, and they washed their feet; and he gave their asses provender.

And they made ready the presents against Joseph came at noon, for they heard that they should eat bread there.

And when Joseph came home, the men brought the presents, and bowed themselves before him to the earth.

And he asked them of their welfare, and said,

Is your father well, the old man, of whom ye spake? is he yet alive? And they bowed their heads and made obeisance.

And he lifted up his eyes and saw his brother Benjamin, his mother's son, and said, Is this your younger brother of whom ye spake unto me? God be gracious unto thee, my son!

And Joseph made haste out; for his love for his brother overcame him; and he sought where to weep, and he entered into his chamber and wept there.

And he washed his face and went back, and refrained himself, and said, Set on bread.

And they set on for him by himself, and for the Egyptians that were with him by themselves, because the Egyptians might not eat bread with the Hebrews.

And they sat before him, the firstborn according to his birthright, and the youngest according to his youth. And the men marvelled one at another.

And he sent messes unto them from before him; but Benjamin's mess was five times as much as any of theirs. And they drank and were cheerful with him.

And he commanded the steward of the house, saying, Fill their sacks with food, as much as they can carry, and put every man's money in his sack's mouth.

And put my cup, the silver cup, in the sack of the youngest, and the corn money. And he did according to the word that Joseph had spoken.

As soon as the morning was light, the men were sent away, they and their asses.

And when they were gone out of the city, and not yet far off, Joseph said unto his steward, Up, follow after the men; and when thou dost overtake them say unto them,

Wherefore have ye rewarded evil for good? Is not this it, in which my lord drinketh? Ye have done evil in so doing.

And he overtook them, and spake unto them the same words.

And they said unto him, Wherefore saith my lord these words; God forbid that thy servants should do according to that thing.

Behold the money which we found in our sacks' mouths, we brought again unto thee, out of the land of Canaan. How then should we steal out of thy lord's house silver or gold?

With whomsoever of thy servants it be found, both let him die, and we also will be my lord's bondmen.

And he said, Let it be according to your words. He with whom it is found shall be my servant, and ye shall be blameless.

Then they speedily took down every man his sack and opened it.

And he searched, beginning at the eldest; and the cup was found in Benjamin's sack.

Then they rent their clothes, and returned to the city, after loading their asses.

And they all came to Joseph's house, and fell before him on the ground.

And Joseph said unto them, What is this deed that ye have done? Knew ye not that I could divine?

And Judah said, What shall we say unto my lord, or how shall we clear ourselves? God hath found out the sin of thy servants.

Behold, we are my lord's servants, both we and he with whom the cup was found.

And Joseph said, God forbid that I should do so; but the man, in whose hand the cup was found, he shall be my servant.

And as for you, get ye up in peace to your father.

CONVERSATION XXVIII.

———o———

Mamma.—Why did Jacob's sons refuse to go a second time into Egypt unless their father would consent that Benjamin should accompany them?

Esther.—Because Joseph had solemnly sworn that they should see his face no more, unless their brother were with them.

Mamma.—What did Jacob say when his sons repeated what Joseph had said, and told him that they would not go into Egypt without Benjamin?

Esther.—He said, "Wherefore dealt ye so ill with me as to tell the man that ye had yet another brother."

Ada.—We do not read that Joseph asked them "If they had yet another brother;" therefore, they did not tell the truth when they said so to their father. Did they, dear Mamma?

Mamma.—We certainly do not read these exact words; but it is quite possible Joseph might have asked them about their brother, or they may have thought that he did so. I do not think in this instance they told an intentional falsehood to their father; they certainly could not know, as they said, that Joseph would desire to see their brother. And further, I wish you to observe, that although every word in our Bible is true, much more must have happened to every individual than is related in it. Moses only wrote down such events as had some relation to the future history of the Jewish people, or contained some lesson by which we were to be benefited.

Ada.—I had not thought of this before, dear Mamma, but it is quite clear to me now. Of course many more events must have happened than we read of.

Mamma.—Did Jacob at last consent that Benjamin should accompany his brethren?

Esther.—Yes; and Judah promised that he would ensure his safe return.

Mamma.—What did Joseph's brothers take with them besides the money which they had found in their sacks?

Esther.—More money to buy corn, and a present for Joseph, of balm, honey, almonds, spices, myrrh, and nuts.

Mamma.—When Joseph perceived Benjamin with his brethren, what did he desire of his steward?

Esther.—He told his steward to bring them into his house that they might eat with him at noon.

Mamma.—How did they feel when they were brought into the house?

Esther.—They were afraid, and thought they were brought there on account of the money that they had found in their sacks.

Mamma.—How did the steward answer when they told him of the money they had found?

Esther.—He said, "Fear not; your God and the God of your father hath given you treasure in your sacks. I had your money."

Mamma.—What further was done that reassured them?

Esther.—Simeon was brought out to them.

Mamma.—When Joseph came home what did his brothers do?

Esther.—They bowed themselves before him to the ground, and brought him the presents which they had prepared for him.

Mamma.—Thus you see Joseph's dreams were fulfilled, his brethren actually bowed down before him. What was the first question Joseph asked of his brethren?

Esther.—He asked if their father was well.

Mamma.—What are we told of Joseph when he saw Benjamin, the son of his own mother?

Esther.—That he could restrain his feelings no longer, but retired to his room to weep.

Mamma.—How did Joseph excite the wonder of his brothers?

Esther.—By placing them at table according to their ages.

Ada.—Why should Joseph have given Benjamin five times as much as his other brethren; he surely could not eat more than they?

Mamma.—It is not necessary to imagine that Joseph's brothers ate all that was placed before them; it is the custom in the East, even in the present day, to give a greater variety of food to the guest who is most honoured, merely as a mark of distinction, in the same way as we should endeavour to procure some rare dish, if we invited to our table a guest to whom we wished to show particular favour.

Ada.—Mamma, does it not appear very unnecessary that Joseph should have had the cup put into Benjamin's sack, to cause his brothers to be brought back again? Might he not have told them at once that he was their brother?

Mamma.—I think he wished to be quite sure of their affection for Benjamin, and to prove that they would not be jealous of him, and treat Benjamin as he had been treated by them himself.

Ada.—O yes, I have no doubt now that this was his reason. I am so glad that you have explained this, dear Mamma, for I did not like to think that Joseph could be unkind and revengeful.

Mamma.—How did Joseph's brothers act when they were overtaken and accused of the theft?

Esther.—They immediately took down the sacks, and desired that they should be searched.

Mamma.—Thus proving that they had no doubt of their own, or of each others' integrity. Do you remember that they all offered to become Joseph's slaves, if the cup should be found with them?

Esther.—Yes, and when it was found in Benjamin's sack, they all rent their clothes and returned with him to Joseph.

Mamma.—What did Judah say when he came into Joseph's presence?

Esther.—He said, " What shall we say unto my lord or

how shall we clear ourselves? God hath found out the sin of thy servants; behold we are my lord's servants, both we and he with whom the cup was found."

Mamma.—How did Joseph answer them?

Esther.—He said, "The man with whom the cup is found shall be my servant. And as for you, get ye up to your father in peace."

READING XXIX.

THEN Judah came near, and said,

O my lord, let thy servant, I pray thee, speak a word in my lord's ears, and let not thine anger burn against thy servant; for thou art even as Pharaoh.

My lord asked thy servants, saying, Have ye a father and a brother?

And we said unto my lord, We have a father, an old man, and a child of his old age, a little one; and his brother is dead, and he alone is left of his mother, and his father loveth him.

And thou saidst unto thy servants, Bring him down unto me, that I may see him.

And we said unto my lord, The lad cannot leave his father; for if he should his father would die.

And thou saidst unto thy servants, Except your youngest brother come with you, ye shall see my face no more.

And it came to pass that when we were come up to thy servant, my father, we told him the words of my lord.

And our father said, Go again, and buy us a little food.

And we said, We cannot go down except our youngest brother be with us, else we cannot see the man's face.

And thy servant, my father, said unto us, Ye know that my wife bare me two sons : and the one went out from me, and I said, Surely he is torn in pieces; and I have not seen him since.

And if ye take this one also from me, and mischief

befall him, ye shall bring down my grey hairs with sorrow to the grave.

Now, therefore, when I come to thy servant, my father, and the lad be not with us (seeing that his life is bound up in the life of the lad),

And it shall come to pass when he seeth that the lad is not with us that he will die; and thy servant shall bring down the grey hairs of thy servant, our father, with sorrow to the grave.

For thy servant became surety for the lad unto my father, saying, If I bring him not unto thee, then I shall bear the blame to my father for ever.

Now, therefore, I pray thee, let thy servant abide (instead of the lad) a bondman to my lord, and let the lad go up with his brethren.

For how shall I go up to my father and the lad be not with me, lest I see the evil that shall come on my father?

Then Joseph could not refrain himself before all those who stood before him;

And he cried, Cause every man to go out from me; and there stood no man with him but his brethren while he made himself known unto them.

And he wept aloud, and the Egyptians and the house of Pharaoh heard.

And he said, I am Joseph your brother, whom ye sold into Egypt,

Come near to me, I pray you; and they came near, but could not answer him, for they were grieved.

And Joseph said, Be not grieved nor angry with yourselves that you sold me hither; for God sent me before you to preserve life.

So now it was not you, but God who sent me hither. And He made me a father unto Pharaoh, and lord of all his house, and ruler over all the land of Egypt.

For these two years hath the famine been in the

land; and yet there are five years in which there shall be neither earing nor harvest.

Haste ye, and go down to my father, and say to him, Thus saith thy son Joseph:

God hath made me lord of all Egypt; come down to me, and tarry not; and thou shalt dwell in the land of Goshen, and thou shalt be near unto me, thou, and thy children, and thy children's children, and thy flocks, and thy herds, and thy goats, and all that thou hast.

And there will I nourish thee; for yet there are five years of famine; lest thou, and thy household, come to poverty.

And, behold, your eyes see, and the eyes of my brother Benjamin, that it is my mouth that speaketh unto you.

And ye shall tell my father of all my glory in Egypt, and of all that ye have seen; and ye shall haste and bring down my father thither.

And Joseph fell upon his brother Benjamin's neck, and wept; and Benjamin wept upon his neck.

Moreover he kissed all his brethren, and wept upon them; and after that his brethren talked with him.

And the report was heard in Pharaoh's house, saying, Joseph's brethren are come; and it was pleasing in the eyes of Pharaoh, and in the eyes of his servants also.

And Pharaoh said unto Joseph, Say unto thy brethren, This do ye; load your beasts, and go, get you into the land of Canaan, and take your father and your households, and come unto me;

And I will give you the best of the land of Egypt, and ye shall eat the fat of the land. Now thou art commanded, this do.

Then Joseph said, Take you wagons out of the land of Egypt for your wives, and for your little ones, and bring your father, and come; also regard not your goods; for the best of all the land of Egypt is yours.

And the children of Israel did so; and Joseph gave them wagons, according to the command of Pharaoh, and gave them provision for the way.

To each of them he gave a change of raiment; but to Benjamin he gave three hundred pieces of silver, and five changes of raiment.

And to his father Joseph sent after this manner: ten asses laden with the good things of Egypt, and ten she asses laden with corn, and bread, and meat for his father by the way.

So he sent his brethren away, and they departed.

And he said unto them, See that ye fall not out by the way.

And they went up out of Egypt, and came into the land of Canaan unto Jacob their father, and told him, Joseph is yet alive, and he is ruler over all the land of Egypt.

And Jacob's heart fainted, for he believed them not. And they told him all the words of Joseph, which he had said unto them.

And when he saw the wagons which Joseph had sent to carry him, his spirit revived;

And he said, It is enough; Joseph my son is yet alive: I will go and see him before I die.

CONVERSATION XXIX.

Mamma.—I should like you, Esther, my dear, to learn to repeat Judah's speech, for it is very beautiful. I think Ada can do so, and she will help you to learn it.

Ada.—Yes, dear Mamma, I know it quite perfectly, and yet every time I repeat it I like it better. It is not surprising that Joseph could restrain his feelings no longer, after this touching appeal in behalf of his brother.

Mamma.—This speech must have reassured him with regard to any feelings he might have imagined that his brethren entertained towards Benjamin. What did he say to them, after he had made himself known unto them, and they appeared grieved and troubled?

Ada.—He said, " Be not grieved, nor angry with yourselves, that you sent me hither; for God sent me before you to preserve you in the earth, and to save your lives."

Mamma.—Do you understand what Joseph meant by this?

Ada.—He meant to prove to his brethren that he bore them no ill will on account of the sufferings they had caused him, but that he looked upon all that had happened as the will of God, and thought that God had purposely allowed him to be sent into Egypt, in order that he might interpret Pharaoh's dreams, and provide against the ill effects of the famine.

Esther.—But do you think, Mamma, Joseph was right to say this,—was it not very wrong of his brothers to sell him into Egypt?

Mamma.—It was undoubtedly a most wicked act, on the part of Joseph's brethren, to sell him into Egypt, but God had turned their evil intentions into good; and it was generous and kind of Joseph to try to console them in this manner, for they appear to have been sincerely penitent.

How did Joseph tell his brethren God had placed him with regard to Pharaoh?

Esther.—He said, " God had made him a father to Pharaoh."

Ada.—Does it not appear strange that Joseph should have remained so long ruler of Egypt before he let his father know of his prosperity?

Mamma.—It would be very strange for a dutiful son to act in such a manner in times like these; but you must remember that in those days there were no regular means of remitting intelligence; he might also have wished to conceal his advancement from his father until he felt himself quite established in Pharaoh's favour, which he could not be certain of until the second part of his predictions came to pass.

Ada.—But why do you think he could not have sent for his father and brethren at first?

Mamma.—He might have imagined that, had he done so, Pharaoh might have doubted the truth of his prophecies, and have thought that he invented the interpretation with cunning, so that he might accomplish the aggrandisement of himself and his family; but mind, my dear children, I merely offer these views as suggestions : we cannot positively know more of the motives of our Biblical characters than our Bible tells us. Whatever may have been Joseph's motives for the manner in which he acted, I cannot believe that he was other than a good and dutiful child and a kind forgiving brother. Esther, my dear, what did Joseph desire of his brethren as soon as he had made himself known unto them?

Esther.—That they would make haste and return to the land of Canaan to fetch his father.

Mamma.—Where did he promise they should dwell?

Esther.—In the land of Goshen.

Mamma.—Have you noticed that it was at Pharaoh's command that Joseph sent wagons to his father to fetch the women and children? and that Pharaoh gave him permission to send whatever he pleased for them?

Ada.—I did not notice this at first, and wondered how Joseph had so much to send for them, and if he were acting quite fairly to do so.

Mamma.—It would appear that he sent nothing but what was strictly his own, until he had Pharaoh's commands to do so. Did Jacob believe his sons when they told him Joseph was alive?

Esther.—Not immediately; but when he saw the wagons which Joseph had sent, his spirit revived.

Mamma.—What did he then say?

Esther.—He said, "It is enough; Joseph my son is yet alive: I will go and see him before I die."

READING XXX.

AND Israel took his journey with all that he had, and came to Beersheba, and offered sacrifice unto the God of his father Isaac.

And God spake unto Israel in visions of the night, and said, Jacob! Jacob! and he said, Here am I.

And he said, I am God, the God of thy father: fear not to go down into Egypt, for I will there make of thee a great nation. I will go down with thee into Egypt, and I will surely bring thee up again; and Joseph shall put his hand upon thine eyes.

And Jacob rose up from Beersheba, and the sons of Israel carried Jacob their father, and their wives, and their little ones, in the wagons which Pharaoh had sent to carry them.

And they took their cattle and their goods, and came into Egypt, Jacob and all his seed with him. All the souls that came with Jacob into Egypt were threescore and ten.

And he sent Judah before him unto Joseph, and they came into the land of Goshen.

And Joseph made ready his chariot, and went up to meet Israel his father, to Goshen; and presented himself unto him, and he fell on his neck and wept awhile.

And Israel said unto Joseph, Now let me die, since I have seen thy face, because thou art yet alive.

And Joseph said unto his brethren and unto his father's house, I will go up and show Pharaoh my brethren and my father's house which are come to me.

And it shall come to pass when Pharaoh shall say, What is your business? that ye shall say, Thy servants have been owners of cattle from our youth even until now, both we and our fathers: that ye may dwell in the land of Goshen.

Then Joseph came and told Pharaoh that his father and his brethren, and their flocks and herds and all that they had, were come out of Canaan into the land of Egypt, and were in the land of Goshen: and he took five of his brethren and presented them unto Pharaoh.

And Pharaoh said unto them, What is your business? And they answered, Thy servants are shepherds, both we, and also our fathers.

And to sojourn in the land are we come; for thy servants have no pasture for their flocks, the famine being sore in the land of Canaan; now therefore, we pray thee, let thy servants dwell in the land of Goshen.

And Pharaoh spake unto Joseph, saying, Thy father and thy brethren are come unto thee; the land of Egypt is before thee, in the best of the land make them to dwell, and make some of them rulers over my cattle.

And Joseph brought in Jacob his father, and set him before Pharaoh. And Jacob blessed Pharaoh.

And Pharaoh said unto Jacob, How old art thou? And Jacob said, The days of the years of my pilgrimage are an hundred and thirty years.

Few and evil have the days of the years of my life been, and I have not attained to the days of the years of the life of my fathers, in the days of their pilgrimage.

And he again blessed Pharaoh, and went out from before him.

And Joseph gave his father and his brethren a possession in Rameses, in the best of the land of Egypt, as Pharaoh had commanded.

And Joseph nourished his father and his brethren, and all their household with bread.

And Joseph gathered up all the money that was found in the land of Egypt, and in the land of Canaan, for the corn which was bought; and Joseph brought the money into Pharaoh's house.

And when all the money failed, the people came to Joseph, and said, Give us bread, for why should we die in thy presence; for the money faileth.

And Joseph said, Give your cattle, if the money fail. And they brought their cattle unto Joseph, and he gave them bread for horses and for cattle, and for flocks and for herds, and for asses; and for these he fed them with bread all that year.

Then came they unto him the next year, and said, We will not hide it from my lord, how that our money is spent. My lord hath also all our beasts, and there is nothing left in the sight of my lord but our bodies and our lands.

Wherefore should we die, and our land also, before thine eyes: buy us and our land for bread, and we and our land will be servants unto Pharaoh.

And Joseph bought all the land of Egypt for Pharaoh, only the land of the priests bought he not, and they did eat of the portion which Pharaoh gave them.

And he removed the people to cities, from the end of the borders of Egypt, and he gave them seed for the land, and in the increase they were to give the fifth part to Pharaoh, and take the rest for food.

And they said, Thou hast saved our lives; let us

find grace in the sight of my lord, and we will be Pharaoh's servants.

And Joseph made it a law over the land of Egypt unto this day, that Pharaoh should have the fifth part, except the land of the priests only, which became not Pharaoh's.

CONVERSATION XXX.

Mamma.—Where did God appear to Jacob, during his journey to Egypt?

Esther.—At Beersheba.

Mamma.—What did God say to him there?

Esther.—He said, "Fear not to go down into Egypt, for I will there make of thee a great nation; I will go down with thee into Egypt, and will surely bring thee up again."

Ada.—But, Mamma, Jacob never left Egypt again.

Mamma.—My dear child, you have fallen into the same error as many persons do, that of taking one verse of the Bible and giving it your own interpretation; God's promise to bring Jacob up again from Egypt never could have been understood as relating to himself, but to his descendants, for it is followed by the words, "And Joseph shall put his hand upon thine eyes."

Ada.—What does that mean, Mamma?

Mamma.—It is an expression used figuratively, to imply that Joseph should be with Jacob when he died; and alludes to the custom of closing the eyes after death. Now as Joseph was ruler over Egypt, it is evident that Jacob did not think that he with all his family would leave Egypt again during his lifetime. How did Joseph meet his father?

Esther.—He went up to him to Goshen and fell on his neck and wept.

Mamma.—How many persons went down with Jacob into Egypt?

Esther.—Seventy.

Mamma.—What did Joseph wish his father and brothers to tell Pharaoh concerning their trade?

Esther.—He wished them to let him know that they

were shepherds, in order that Pharaoh might give them the land of Goshen to dwell in.

Ada.—Do you think Joseph had any special reason for wishing his brethren to inhabit that part of the country?

Mamma.—Yes, I think he might have had more than one reason; firstly, it would appear that the land of Goshen was best suited for pasturing their cattle, and secondly, it is likely that Joseph thought it better to separate his family from the people of the land, lest they might disagree on account of the differences of their customs. The Israelites used animals for food which the Egyptians regarded as sacred. You should understand this, Ada, from having read the history of ancient Egypt, but Esther is too young to do so. How many of his brethren did Joseph present to Pharaoh?

Esther.—Five.

Mamma.—What do we read of Jacob when he came into Pharaoh's presence?

Esther.—That he blessed Pharaoh.

Mamma.—How did he answer when Pharaoh asked him concerning his age?

Ada.—He said, "The days of the years of my pilgrimage are an hundred and thirty years; few and evil have the days of the years of my life been; and I have not attained to the days of the years of the life of my fathers in the days of their pilgrimage."

Esther.—Mamma, dear, what does Jacob mean by "the years of my pilgrimage?"

Mamma.—A pilgrimage means a journey; it would appear, therefore, that Jacob looked upon this life only as a preparation for another state of existence. What employment did Pharaoh desire Joseph to give his brothers?

Esther.—He desired him to make some of them rulers over his cattle.

Mamma.—What did Joseph tell the people to bring in exchange for bread when their money was expended?

Esther.—Firstly their cattle, then their lands and themselves.

Mamma.—What arrangement did Joseph make with them?

Ada.—He gave them seed for the land on condition that they should give a fifth of the increase to Pharaoh.

Mamma.—Which of Pharaoh's subjects were exempt from this tax?

Esther.—The priests.

READING XXXI.

AND Israel lived in the land of Egypt seventeen years, in the country of Goshen; and they had possessions therein, and increased greatly.

And the time drew near that Israel must die: and he called his son Joseph and said unto him,

If now I have found grace in thy sight, put, I pray thee, thy hand under my thigh, and deal kindly and truly with me; bury me not, I pray thee, in Egypt: but I will lie with my fathers; and thou shalt carry me out of Egypt, and bury me in their burying-place.

And Joseph said, I will do as thou hast said.

And he said, Swear unto me, and he sware unto him. And Israel bowed himself upon the bed.

And it came to pass after these things, Joseph heard that his father was sick, and he took his two sons, Manasseh and Ephraim. And one told Jacob, Behold thy son Joseph cometh unto thee.

And Israel raised himself, and sat upon the bed, and said unto Joseph, God Almighty appeared unto me at Luz, in the land of Canaan, and blessed me; and said unto me,

Behold, I will make thee fruitful, and multiply thee, and I will make of thee a great people, and will give this land to thy seed after thee for ever.

And now thy two sons Ephraim and Manasseh, which were born unto thee, in the land of Egypt, are mine: as Reuben and Simeon they shall be mine.

And Israel beheld Joseph's sons, and said, Who are these?

And Joseph said unto his father, They are my sons, whom God hath given me in this place.

And Jacob said, Bring them, I pray thee, unto me, and I will bless them. Now the eyes of Israel were dim, and he could not see.

And Joseph brought them near, and he kissed and embraced them.

And Israel said unto Joseph, I had not thought to see thy face, and lo! God hath shewn me also thy seed.

And Joseph brought them to him, and bowed himself before him to the earth.

And Joseph took Ephraim, in his right hand, towards Israel's left hand, and Manasseh in his left hand, towards Israel's right hand, and brought them near unto him.

And Israel stretched out his right hand, and laid it upon Ephraim's head, who was the younger, and his left hand upon Manasseh's, guiding his hands wittingly.

And Israel blessed Joseph, and said, The God before whom my fathers Abraham and Isaac walked, the God who fed me from my first being unto this day, The angel who redeemed me from all evil, bless the lads; and let my name be called on them, and the name of my fathers Abraham and Isaac, and let them grow into a multitude in the midst of the earth.

And when Joseph saw that his father laid his right hand upon the head of Ephraim, it displeased him; and he held up his hand, to remove it to Manasseh's head, and said,

Not so my father: for this is the firstborn, put thy right hand upon his head. But his father refused, and said,

I know it, my son, I know it: he also shall become a people, and he also shall be great, but truly his brother shall be greater than he, and his seed shall become a multitude of nations.

And he blessed them that day, saying, In thee, shall Israel bless, saying, God make thee as Ephraim and Manasseh. And he set Ephraim before Manasseh.

And Israel said unto Joseph, Behold I die: but God shall be with you and bring you again into the land of your fathers.

Moreover, I have given thee one portion above thy brethren, which I took out of the hand of the Amorite with my sword and with my bow.

CONVERSATION XXXI.

Mamma.—When Israel felt that his end was drawing near, what request did he make of Joseph?

Esther.—That he would not bury him in the land of Egypt, but would take him and bury him in the burying place of his fathers, in the land of Canaan.

Mamma.—Do you remember the name of this burying place? and who else were already buried there?

Esther.—Yes, it was called the cave of Machpelah. And in it were already buried, Sarah, Abraham, Isaac, Rebekah, and Leah.

Mamma.—When Joseph heard that his father was ill, what did he do?

Esther.—He took his two sons Manasseh and Ephraim and went to visit him.

Mamma.—How did Joseph behave when he entered his father's presence?

Esther.—He bowed himself before him to the ground. Was not this a very strange way of saluting his father?

Mamma.—It is the usual manner, in eastern countries, of saluting a superior. The relation of this little incident may have more meaning than we think of at a first reading. It appears to me that the intention of Moses, our lawgiver, when he transcribed these words, was to shew us that although Joseph was in a position of much greater power than his father, he still acknowledged his father's superiority, so he bowed himself humbly before him when he entered his presence; thus teaching us, that, however superior to his parents a child may become, either in worldly possessions or knowledge, he should always behave himself humbly and respectfully towards them.

Esther.—Why did Jacob place Ephraim before Manasseh? We do not read that Manasseh had done anything wrong.

Mamma.—I cannot give you a reason for Jacob's preference of the younger to the elder. There may have been some reason which is not given us, but it is evident that Jacob's blessings were all prophetic, and not regulated by his own wishes. We cannot question God's reasons, if things have occurred that do not appear just to our minds, we must trust to our Creator and feel sure that he is wiser and more just than we are.

Esther.—What do you mean, Mamma, by saying that all Jacob's blessings were prophetic?

Mamma.—I mean, my dear, that they related to events which were to occur at a future period. You will understand this better after our conversation on the next chapter. Can you, Ada, repeat the words in which Jacob blessed Ephraim and Manasseh?

Ada.—He said, "The God who fed me all my life long, unto this day, the angel who redeemed me from all evil, bless the lads; and let my name be named on them and the names of my fathers Abraham and Isaac; and let them grow into a multitude in the midst of the earth."

Mamma.—Was there not something more that Jacob said in blessing them?

Ada.—Yes, he said, "In thee shall Israel bless, saying, God make thee as Ephraim and Manasseh."

Mamma.—Have you remarked that this is the oldest form of prayer we have on record?

Esther.—How do you mean, Mamma? when you and Papa bless us on שבת (Shabbos) evening, you are not saying prayers.

Mamma.—Yes, my darling, we are praying God, to give you His blessing. A human blessing is of no value unless it is made effective by God; indeed, it is almost a mistake to say that a parent blesses his child. He only prays God to do so, the words are, "may God make thee like," etc.

Esther.—Thank you, dear Mamma; I understand this now; but what do you mean by calling this the oldest form of prayer? Have you not told us that Abraham and many others prayed to God?

Mamma.—Yes, my dear; undoubtedly they did. I did not say this was the oldest prayer on record, but the oldest *form* of prayer, by which I meant that it is the first of which we have the words given, and these words have been handed down from father to son, and are used by us at the present day, although it is more than three thousand years since Jacob spoke them.

Esther.—This is indeed wonderful, dear Mamma.

Mamma.—I wish you to remark it, not so much as being wonderful, but that you may think of the great antiquity of the Jewish people, and remember that we were a distinct nation hundreds of years before any of the nations of modern Europe existed.

READING XXXII.

—o—

AND Jacob called unto his sons, and said, Gather yourselves together, that I may tell you that which shall befall you in days to come.

Gather yourselves together, and hear, ye sons of Jacob, and hearken unto Israel, your father.

Reuben, thou art my firstborn, my might and the beginning of my strength; unstable as water, thou shalt not excel.

Simeon and Levi are brethren; instruments of cruelty are their swords. My soul shall not come into their secret; I will divide them in Jacob, and scatter them in Israel.

Judah, thou art he whom thy brethren shall praise; thy hand shall be on the neck of thine enemies, thy father's children shall bow down before thee.

Judah is a lion's whelp; from the prey, my son, thou risest up. The staff shall not depart from Judah nor the lawgiver from between his feet, until he cometh to Shiloh, and his be the obedience of nations.*

He bindeth his foal to the vine, and his ass's colt unto the choice vine; he washeth his garments in wine and his clothes in the blood of grapes. His eyes shall be red with wine, and his teeth white with milk.

Zebulun shall dwell at the margin of the sea; and he shall be for a haven of ships; and his border shall be unto Zidon.

* See De Sola, Lindenthal, and Dr. Raphael, p. 329, note 10 on chap. xlix. 10.

Issachar is a strong ass crouching down between the stables. And he saw the resting place that it was good and the land that it was pleasant; and he bowed his shoulder to bear, and became a servant unto tribute.

Dan shall judge his people as one of the tribes of Israel. Dan shall be a serpent by the way, an adder in the path, that biteth the horse in the heels, so that his rider falleth backward.

For thy salvation I hope, O Lord!

Gad, a troop shall overcome him, but he shall overcome at last.

Out of Asher cometh fat bread, and he shall yield royal dainties.

Naphtali is a hind let loose; he giveth good words.

Joseph is a fruitful bough, even a fruitful bough by a well, whose branches hang over the wall. The archers have sorely grieved him and shot at him, and hated him; but his bow abode in strength, and the arms of his hand were made strong by the hands of the mighty God of Jacob, from thence thou becamest the shepherd, the stone of Israel.

From the God of thy father, who shall help thee, and from the Almighty who shall bless thee with blessings of heaven above, and of the deep beneath, and with the blessing of a multitude of children.

With the blessings of thy father that have excelled the blessings of my forefathers unto the utmost bowels of the everlasting hills: these shall be upon the head of Joseph, and on the crown of the head of him who was separated from his brethren.

Benjamin shall be as a ravenous wolf; in the morning he shall devour the prey, and at night he shall divide the spoil.

All these are the twelve tribes of Israel. And this is the blessing wherewith he blessed them.

And he charged them to bury him in the cave of Machpelah, the cave which Abraham had bought of Ephron the Hittite, and where Abraham, Sarah, Isaac, Rebekah and Leah were buried.

And when Jacob had made an end of speaking, he gathered up his feet into the bed; he yielded up his spirit, and was gathered unto his people.

And Joseph fell upon his father's face, and wept and kissed him.

And Joseph commanded the physicians to embalm his father, and they did so.

And forty days were fulfilled for him, for so do they for those who are embalmed.

And the Egyptians mourned for Israel seventy days.

And when the days of his mourning were past, Joseph sent to Pharaoh, saying, My father made me swear, saying, Lo, I die; in my grave which I have digged for me in the land of Canaan, there shalt thou bury me.

Now, therefore, let me go up, I pray thee, and bury my father, and I will return again.

And Pharaoh said, Go up and bury thy father.

And Joseph went, and with him went all the servants of Pharaoh, the elders of his house, and all the elders of the land of Egypt, and all the house of Joseph, and his brethren and his father's house; only their little ones, their flocks, and their herds, they left in the land of Goshen.

And there went up with Joseph a great company of Egyptians, chariots, and horsemen, and they came to the threshing-floor of Atad, which is beyond the river Jordan. And there they mourned for Jacob seven days.

And when the people of Canaan saw the mourning, they said, This is a grievous mourning to the

Egyptians: wherefore the name of the place was called Abel Mitzraim.

And Jacob's sons buried him, as he had commanded them, in the cave of Machpelah.

And Joseph and his brethren returned to Egypt.

And after Jacob's death, Joseph's brethren said, Peradventure Joseph will now hate us, and will requite us all the evil we did unto him.

And they sent to Joseph, saying, Thy father commanded before he died, saying, So shall ye say to Joseph.

Forgive now, I pray thee, the trespass of thy brethren, and their sin, for they did thee evil, and now we pray thee, forgive the trespass of the servants of the God of thy father.

And Joseph wept when they spake unto him; and his brethren also wept and fell down before his face, and they said, Behold, we are thy servants.

And Joseph said, Fear not; am I in the place of God?

But as for you, ye thought to do me evil, but God meant it unto good, to bring to pass as it is this day, to save many people alive.

Now, therefore, fear ye not; I will nourish you and your little ones. And he comforted them, and spake kindly unto them.

And Joseph dwelt in Egypt, he and his father's house; and Joseph lived an hundred and ten years.

And Joseph saw Ephraim's children of the third generation; the children also of Machir, the son of Manasseh, were brought up upon Joseph's knees.

And Joseph said to his brethren, I die: and God will surely visit you, and bring you out of this land unto the land which He sware unto Abraham, Isaac, and Jacob.

And Joseph took an oath of the children of Israel, saying, God will surely visit you, and ye shall carry up my bones from here.

So Joseph died, being an hundred and ten years old, and they embalmed him, and he was put in a coffin in Egypt.

CONVERSATION XXXII.

Mamma.—For what purpose did Jacob call his sons together?

Esther.—To give them his blessing before he died.

Mamma.—You are right as to fact, my dear, but these are not the words of the text, nor all that Jacob's blessing implied.

Esther.—Oh! I remember, Mamma; it was to tell them what should happen in days to come.

Mamma.—To what period do Jacob's prophecies mostly relate?

Ada.—To the period when the children of Israel should be settled in the land of Canaan.

Mamma.—Can you tell me by what other names the land of Canaan is often called?

Ada.—Yes, it is sometimes called the promised land, and sometimes Palestine, or the Holy Land.

Esther.—Is it called the promised land because it was promised to the children of Israel by God?

Mamma.—Yes, my dear, and the Holy Land because it is the land to which the Bible history relates. Palestine is a proper name; it is not uncommon for places to have two proper names.

Esther.—Mamma dear, I do not understand the meaning of the blessings Jacob gave his sons.

Mamma.—I did not expect that you would, my dear, without explanation. Some you are too young to understand at present, and of others the meaning is not quite clear even to people who have studied deeply. When you are older, you shall read all we know about them. What I wish to impress upon your memory is, never to believe any interpretations that may be given you by strangers; by this I mean, by people of other creeds, or even by those f our own, who have not sufficiently studied the subject. The language, which is figurative, is very difficult for an English child to understand, for we are not used to figures of speech.

Esther.—What do you mean by figurative language, dear Mamma?

Mamma.—By figurative language is meant, language in which objects are used to express qualities or circumstances. Thus we read Joseph is a fruitful bough; you know very well, that we are not to imagine that Joseph was the branch of a tree. This means that Joseph should be likened to a branch which bore many leaves, alluding to the multitude of children promised him; thus also, when we read the archers shot at him, this is not intended literally, but as alluding to the troubles which his brothers had caused him. I should like you to learn to repeat the blessings, all of them if you can, or if that is too much, at least the blessing of Joseph.

Esther.—I will, my dear Mamma.

Mamma.—Where did Jacob desire to be buried?

Esther.—In the cave of Machpelah.

Mamma.—How many days did the Egyptians mourn for Jacob?

Esther.—Seventy.

Mamma.—What did Joseph order to be done to Jacob's body?

Esther.—He ordered the king's physicians to embalm it.

Ada.—Was this right, dear Mamma?

Mamma.—I cannot say whether it was actually right or wrong of Joseph to have his father's body embalmed. Embalming is a purely Egyptian custom. It is evident that Joseph's intention was to give honour to his father's remains, so that the people of the country might acknowledge the respect due to him. Israelites of the present day, would not consider it right to endeavour to preserve the remains of the dead, for God has said, "Dust thou art, and unto dust thou shalt return;" therefore we disturb the dead as little as possible, merely placing them in the earth in a wooden coffin.

Esther.—Mamma, dear, what do you mean by embalming?

Mamma.—It is a process by which the flesh of the dead is preserved for many years. We have now in the British Museum the remains of people who were found buried in Egypt, supposed to be as ancient as the time of Jacob. Do you remember how long ago that is?

Esther.—You told us more than three thousand years.

Mamma.—Who accompanied Joseph into Canaan when he went to bury his father?

Esther.—All his brethren and many of Pharaoh's servants.

Mamma.—Where did they again mourn for Jacob?

Esther.—At the threshing-floor of Atad.

Mamma.—What did the people say when they saw this great mourning?

Esther.—They said, אָבֵל־מִצְרַיִם (O-vel Mitzraim); it is mourning of the Egyptians.

Mamma.—Have you noticed that at the floor of Atad the Israelites mourned again for Jacob seven days after his interment, thus giving him, as it were, the double honours, mourning both in accordance with Egyptian and Israelitish customs.

Ada.—You mean to say then, Mamma, that it was the custom of the Israelites to mourn for seven days as early as the time of Jacob.

Mamma.—It would appear so, since had it not been a usual custom to mourn seven days as we do now, the Israelites would have been satisfied with the seventy days of mourning in Egypt.

Esther.—Do you think that Jacob really told Joseph's brethren to ask his forgiveness?

Mamma.—I scarcely think so, but it is not of much importance whether he did, or did not. Joseph appears to have been much affected at his brothers' message to him; doubtless he thought they had been sufficiently long with him to have felt confident that he had entirely forgiven them. Do you remember Joseph's answer to them?

Esther.—Yes, Joseph said, "Fear not, for am I in the

place of God? Though you thought evil against me, God meant it unto good, in order to bring to pass as it is to-day, to save many people alive."

Ada.—What did Joseph mean by saying, "Am I in the place of God?"

Mamma.—I think he meant to convey to them that, as far as he was concerned, he had freely forgiven them; but inasmuch as they had sinned against God, it was from Him they must pray for forgiveness. It may be that he wished to show that it would not be right to take upon himself the act of punishment which belongs to God alone. Here is a great lesson, teaching us that we must never seek to punish an enemy. What further promise did Joseph make his brethren?

Esther.—That he would nourish both them and their little ones.

Mamma.—How old was Joseph when he died?

Ada.—One hundred and ten years.

Mamma.—Whom are we told that he lived to see?

Ada.—His great grand-children.

Mamma.—What promise did he exact of the Israelites before he died?

Ada.—That they would carry his bones with them into the land of Canaan, for he firmly believed that God would fulfil the promise He had made to Abraham, Isaac, and Jacob.

www.ingramcontent.com/pod-product-compliance
Lightning Source LLC
Chambersburg PA
CBHW021728220426
43662CB00008B/750